WAS SHAKESPEARE SHAKESPEARE?

Shakespear if Player by Garter

The document, now in the Folger Museum in Washington, that emerged from the quarrel in 1602 in the College of Heralds (see page 77), showing irrefutably that Shakespeare of Stratford and Shakespeare the Player were one and the same man.

WAS SHAKESPEARE SHAKESPEARE?

A Lawyer Reviews

The Evidence

by

Milward W. Martin

COOPER SQUARE PUBLISHERS, INC.

NEW YORK

1 9 6 5

Table of Contents

Introduction

A book on Shakespeare that would completely silence the skeptics who deny the Stratford man's authorship is an impossibility. The skeptics simply refuse to see, and those who refuse to see always continue to be blind.

It is not to them but rather to those of open mind that Mr. Martin has addressed this book, to those who honestly wish to know the incontrovertible story of the authorship, sustained not by surmise and conjecture but by documents of unquestioned authenticity.

In the pages that follow, that is the story that is set forth.

As editor of *The Shakespeare Newsletter* since its inception in 1951, I have found myself from time to time both purposely and inadvertently involved in the authorship arguments, for the skeptics occasionally have at me with their usual religious fervor. The skeptics, I have found, are an extraordinary breed and, strange to say, extraordinarily alike. Listen to one and you have heard them all. Mr. Martin calls them "lotus eaters," and the name is very apt, for, sincere and delightful people that many of them are, they wilfully delude themselves by denying or misconstruing the facts.

They leap chasms, biographical and literary, with an agility that can only astound those with a knowledge of the facts and the impossibility of their claims. Yet this very agility, which genuinely shocks the true scholars, quite often convinces the credulous—and on this subject the general reading public is very largely uninformed. From that, the host of skeptics grows.

They sound forth the sledge-hammer fact that there is absolutely no evidence that Shakespeare of Stratford ever attended school; but do they always tell the uniformed reader that *all* Stratford school records are lost, hence there is no evidence that *anyone* in Stratford at that time attended school? They point to his many legal expressions to prove he must have been a lawyer, which the Stratford man was not; but do they point out how many dramatists of the era used similar phrases, many to a far greater extent than did Shakespeare? They show his six known signatures and claim that no one with such an "illiterate" scrawl could have written those plays; but do they ever admit that he wrote in Elizabethan "secretary" script, common then but non-existent today, and that in that script his handwriting was not "illiterate" at all?

Half-truths, misconceptions, impossible conclusions, "interpretations" that require the un-writing of the plays—these are the skeptics' stock-in-trade. To argue against them is, I have found, pointless. After reading my replies to seventeen questions put to me by leading Baconians (*The Shakespeare Newsletter,* XIII:2, April, 1963), a professional psychiatrist at the University of Chicago wrote me recently:

> "I doubt whether you have converted any heretics. The issue at stake is beyond the reality principle and fulfills emotional needs much as any illusory belief does and thus cannot be influenced by fact and reason."

This is psychoanalytically sound. My experience has told me that in many cases the desire for notoriety is as strong in some heretics as is the desire for truth.

It is the documented evidence that destroys the skeptics; it is on surmises and conjectures that they survive. Hence it is that, one and all, they strive to avoid the documented evidence and move the discussion into the realm of conjecture where they can argue without fear of a crushing rejoinder. As Mr. Martin puts it, all of them ask us to "forget for a while the thing called evidence.

This book will leave many of them frustrated, for Mr. Martin has steadfastly stuck to the documented evidence and steadfastly refused to get into the argumentative field of unsupported surmise and conjecture from which arises so much of the confusion the skeptics succeed in kicking up.

In the pages which follow it will be seen that Mr. Martin, with exceeding good sense and patience, has come to grips with the problem. In page after page of cited facts, he demolishes point by point the usual "evidence" of the skeptics in a manner that should make them realize once and for all the basic untenability of their position. The approximate three dozen sections into which Mr. Martin divides his evidence could have been extended, and the sections lengthened, of course, but Mr. Martin is not writing an encyclopedia. Mr. Martin might also have extended his book by animadversions on the implausibility of the ciphers which would have required Bacon to write his cipher story on large folio sheets and then ingeniously to have written the plays around it. He could have cited some of the numerous parallelisms and shown the universality of the ideas among literate Elizabethans. But he has obviously thought it best not to complicate his discussion with denial of all of the ludicrous arguments of the Baconians, Oxfordians, and others. He has clearly surveyed the material which the skeptics offer as proof and shows unequivocally what the actual evidence is.

To all who would know the documented and incontrovertible story of the authorship, I recommend the pages which follow.

LOUIS MARDER
Editor, The Shakespeare Newsletter
December, 1964

Author's Preface

IT IS largely as an answer to the series of articles published in the *Journal of the American Bar Association* in 1959 and early 1960, and later turned into a book entitled "Shakespeare Cross-Examination," that this present book is written.

Your true Shakespearean buff (and there are millions), whether he credits the authorship of the Shakespearean works to the man from Stratford or to one of the pretenders, feels in his heart a deep sense of personal loyalty to the author of those works, whoever that author may have been. To a man, they intensely want justice done him.

Pro-Stratfordians seethe with indignation at the mention of some pretender's name; anti-Stratfordians have only contempt when the man from Stratford is praised.

On this field of battle the emotions lie close to the surface. Wise hostesses forbid it as dinner party conversation, lest angry name-calling get beyond control.

On one point only do both sides feel alike; and on it they both express themselves with their customary lack of restraint—namely the importance of the question to each supporter personally. In the eyes of every pro-Stratfordian and every anti-Stratfordian alike, if any group in the world is beyond the pale it is that pitiable breed that sometimes chirps up with: "It's only the works themselves that count—not who wrote them." With admirable restraint one can only say: *"Indeed?"*

But the matter moves beyond the field for jest or quip when a publication of the standing of the *Journal of the American Bar Association*, under the aegis of that admirable Association, hands out to the lawyers of America as worthy of their consideration pages of unscholarly stuff and nonsense.

Those articles should be answered, and, as will appear in the pages that follow, to answer them is one of the primary purposes of this book.

WAS SHAKESPEARE SHAKESPEARE?

I

The Lotus Eaters
of Anti-Stratfordia

OF ALL the odd items in the folklore of the Western World, none, probably, is more bizarre than the one that possibly William Shakespeare of Stratford-on-Avon wasn't "Shakespeare" after all.

It has no foundation of documented evidence, that bit of folklore, none to support it having ever been discovered. Yet it has shown a capacity to survive and keep itself in the public eye that is surprising.

It was an idea that came along quite late in the day. If any person during Shakespeare's lifetime so much as whispered such a thought no record that he did so exists. In fact, as the Shakespearean era moved through the 1590s towards the 1600s, and one by one the plays and poems reached the public, the name "William Shakespeare" demonstrably grew to great fame and importance in London's literary and theatrical circles; and since in all that period there was no "William Shakespeare" in the public eye except William Shakespeare the actor from Stratford, the glory, in many, many eyes, could have accrued only to him. Had he been a fraud his fellow actors would have known it. Yet throughout all those years his fellow actors continued, again demonstrably, to work in the theatre with him on the most intimate and friendly terms, with never a sign of jealousy or suspicion. Had he been a fraud this could not have been.

Similarly, the writers of his day referred time and again, during his lifetime, to the beautiful plays and poems of "William Shakespeare," never once indicating that they were referring to some "William Shakespeare" other than the actor from Stratford, the one who was in the public eye.

Thus, if during his lifetime, any actor or writer had wished to indicate that the author and the actor were not one and the same man, the occasions for doing so were legion. Yet not once did any actor or writer, or anyone else, even hint at such a thought. Certainly he could not have fooled them all.

A century and a half after his death, in 1769, one Herbert Lawrence published his *The Life and Adventures of Common Sense,* a mild little allegory in which "Common Sense" (son of Wisdom and Truth) arrived in London in 1588 and proceeded to write the plays which Shakespeare passed off as his own. That little fantasy seems harmless enough, but Baconians have since claimed that "Common Sense" was intended to mean Sir Francis Bacon.

However, no one paid any attention to Mr. Lawrence, and another three-quarters of a century passed. Then, in 1848, one J. C. Hart in his *The Romance of Yachting* wrote that Shakespeare "grew up in ignorance and viciousness and became a common poacher," expressing the very point-of-view that now underlies all anti-Stratfordian thinking, namely, that for Shakespeare of Stratford to have been the author was impossible.

It was in the 1850s that the idea began to gain publicity momentum. In 1856 one W. H. Smith issued his *Bacon and Shakespeare: An Inquiry Touching Players, Playhouses and Play-Writers In the Days of Elizabeth,* declaring his own belief that the Stratford man was illiterate and that Bacon was the author. He was answered in 1857 by one George H. Townsend, who put out a pamphlet entitled *William Shakespeare Not An Imposter*

—and thus the issue was joined. In that same year Delia Bacon, not a relative, published her *The Philosophy of the Plays of Shakespeare Unfolded*, probably the most widely known and least read (it was unconscionably long) of all the earlier anti-Stratfordian books. Miss Bacon seems to have arrived at her conclusion via a mystical revelation; and eventually she was adjudged insane. She is generally regarded as a Baconian, but actually she believed Sir Walter Raleigh gave Bacon a very helping hand.

Thus, really starting in the 1850s, after Shakespeare of Stratford had been more than two centuries dead, the theory that the Stratford man did not write the plays and poems had its origin (and it is important to bear this in mind), not in any discovered evidence, but in the wholly theoretical conviction that he was too illiterate to have done so.

It is that conviction, and nothing more (for documented evidence to support the pretenders is non-existent), that has continued as the basic foundation on which all anti-Stratfordianism rests. "It is *impossible* that that man from *Stratford* was the author"—that is the starting point from which each eager detective takes off on his safari through the jungles of Elizabethan literature in his efforts to demonstrate who the real author was.

Looney, the "discoverer" in 1920 of the Seventeenth Earl of Oxford as the true author, puts the basic tenet this way in his *"Shakespeare" Identified* (p. 49):

"... it is the incredible that Stratfordianism has to face . . ." having already said (p. 36) that "it is impossible to believe" in his authorship.

The *Journal of the American Bar Association*, (hereinafter referred to as *The American Bar Association Journal*), in its issue of November, 1959, p. 1230, states that basic tenet as follows:

> ". . . the Stratfordian authorship appears factually unsupported at best, and moreover seems an utterly incredible paradox—a phenomenon contravening human experience."

There, in those words, we see the foundation stone of anti-Stratfordianism—his authorship is "impossible." The man from Stratford did not have the necessary education; if he revealed any early intimations of poetic or literary talent, nothing is now known of it; he came from a home and family where no such early talent, even had it existed, could possibly have received nourishment; and every known documented fact directly involving him personally shows considerable interest in money but none at all in literary pursuits. Accordingly it is "impossible" that he could have been the world's greatest author; "incredible"—"Contravening human experience."

It is an odd little world, this Anti-Stratfordia, inhabited by many sincere and quite lovely people—but they are self-deluded lotus-eaters, every one. For they have drugged themselves, not with evidence, but with pure theory that his authorship is "impossible."

That is their argument and their basic tenet. Naturally enough, if they deeply believe such a tenet they feel released from considering any contrary evidence showing that he *was* the author. Since it is "impossible," like the cow jumping over the moon, any evidence showing that it did happen, no matter how well documented, is not something to be considered, but merely something to be rationalized away, and is so treated by them. Thus it is that when our anti-Stratfordian friends present dreamt-up fantasies unsupported by evidence, but which rationalize away evidence that is solidly documented, they are not mere special pleaders but are in reality genuine seekers after truth, striving with their unsupported theories to suggest a solution to what they insist is truly a "mystery." Beyond question that is the light in which they see themselves.

In the 1850s, when anti-Stratfordianism really got its start, wide-spread "Bardolatry" had mushroomed to very foolish proportions. Shakespeare worshippers were claiming that their hero from Stratford was a god, possessed of all human knowledge, much of which had to be learned from books, such as knowledge of law, knowledge of medicine, knowledge of foreign languages and of both ancient and modern literature. Coupled with all this, in the 1850s, was the absence of almost any reliable information as to just who the man from Stratford was. They knew he had been born, but of humble origin and with no demonstrable educational advantages; they knew a monument had been erected to him in Stratford—but beyond that and the collected edition of his works in the *First Folio* they knew little else.

Accordingly, when otherwise sensible Baconians began in the 1850s to say it was all a fraud, they found many who were willing at least to listen. True, it was indeed odd that the author of such great literature would, for no demonstrable reason, want to keep his authorship hidden. But to the eager denigrators that presented no problem at all. Since the unknown author had never stated any motive for his secrecy, ingenious Baconians dreamt up motives for him—dreamt them up out of totally whole cloth, and found them, so far as they were concerned, wholly satisfactory.

Many people, as they listened, decided that neither side was supported by really convincing evidence—hence it was at least a "mystery," and, as might be expected, a "mystery" about so intriguing a matter drew shoals of amateur detectives who believed themselves competent to solve it. The literary output steadily grew till it became enormous—and thus it was that the idea that possibly Shakespeare of Stratford wasn't "Shakespeare" received enough publicity to make it stick, at least as an item of western-world folklore.

As more and more amateur detectives joined in the search for a "solution," more and more pretenders began to be "discovered." Up until the end of World War I it was largely Sir Francis Bacon who dominated the field, though other names were mentioned; but around the end of World War I the floodgates opened. As a result, Sir Francis is now merely one in an overcrowded pretenders' field.

For not only was the "mystery" itself stimulating mentally; there were also tangible rewards for almost any kind of clever "solution." Books and articles were accepted for publication (still are) and are widely read and discussed, making each author something of an authority. Thereupon lecture tours, television broadcasts, lionization at cocktail parties all follow as a reward—and largely the audiences are docile, because largely uninformed.

Scholarship ceased to be, if it ever had been, a requirement for announcing a "solution," the chief requirement being a lively and inventive imagination. No one was required to back a pretender already "discovered" by someone else. Any one could, and many did, choose a new pretender to back, using the same arguments for the new one as had already been published for the old, for the theories (and they are merely theories, not evidence) that support one pretender support almost any other equally well. Naturally, the list soon grew to be enormous. At latest count the pretenders "discovered" to date "now number fifty-seven" (Gibson, *The Shakespeare Claimants,* p. 10), and in his *Shakespeare and His Betters* Mr. Churchill lists them all by name, on pages 121 and 122. The literary output in their support, as more and more eager detectives crowd forward for recognition, goes up in almost geometric progression, with books and articles now well into the thousands—till the whole matter has taken on many of the aspects of a mere parlor-game—"Choose Your Own Shakespeare."

A phenomenon such as this definitely calls for analysis.

II

On What Meat Do These Our Anti-Stratfordian Friends Feed?

WHENCE comes this dedicated conviction so universally the hallmark of the anti-Stratfordian? Whence the material that sustains them in their long-continued vigils on the ramparts of Anti-Stratfordia?

It comes not from documented evidence, that is crystal clear. No document of primary evidential value, newly found or old, is ever cited by them. Theories, yes—theories in abundance from lively imaginations; but never evidence. In fact, the solidly documented evidence is ignored or rationalized away.

Almost any anti-Stratfordian book, taken at random, reveals this fact. In one of the most recent, *Shakespeare, The Real Man Behind the Name,* the Ogburns (Oxford supporters) spend many pages telling us how great the "mystery" is, how unlikely was the Stratford man's background, how greatly qualified by birth, education and demonstrated poetic ability was the Seventeenth Earl of Oxford—but no evidence as to the authorship. Other books are similar.

Occasionally "parallelisms" are cited, and hailed as "documentary evidence"—"Parallelisms," where some Shakespearean passage resembles some passage in the works of Bacon,

Oxford, Marlowe or other pretender. This, it is then claimed, "proves" that the Shakespearean passage was written by the pretender. Weakly impotent as this argument is, it breaks down totally when it is shown, as has been many times done, that Shakespearean parallels with Bacon's works are equalled by Shakespearean parallels with Oxford's works and Shakespearean parallels with Marlowe's works. Possibly plagiarism, on one side or the other—but not evidence supporting any pretender.

It is on "negative evidence" that the anti-Stratfordians really base their claims, on numerous small items that arouse their suspicions, coupled with the argument (un-supported by one scintilla of evidence) that the eye-witnesses who stated that the Stratford man was the author may possibly have been lying for pay.

Their "evidence," really merely arguments, to be culled from hundreds if not thousands of books, can be summarized as follows:

1. That it is impossible that that Stratford man could have been the author, for:

   (a) He lacked the necessary education;

   (b) He showed no signs, so far as is known, of any early poetic talent;

   (c) His name was not "Shakespeare," it was Shaksper";

   (d) His dealings in grain and real estate in Stratford, and his litigations there for small sums, show too great an interest in money for him to have been the great poet;

   (e) His contemporary writers never, in his liftetime, referred to any "Shakespeare of Stratford"; they merely wrote in praise of "Shakespeare," hence could have been referring to someone other than the Stratford man;

   (f) The many legal terms in the Shakespearean works

10

show that the author must have been a lawyer, which the Stratford man was not;

(g) If he was ever paid for the plays, no evidence of such payment has ever been discovered;

(h) He took no interest in the publication of the plays and made no mention of them in his will;

(i) No letter written by him is known to exist, and only one written to him, a letter seeking a loan;

(j) He was a commoner who could not have had the familiarity with life in the royal court, or with falconry and other regal sports, which the plays seem to show;

(k) He could not have had the knowledge of classic literature or of foreign countries indicated in the plays;

(l) As a commoner he would not have dared write so disparagingly, at times, of the royal family's ancestors, lest Queen Elizabeth crack him down;

(m) The manuscripts of all the works have disappeared, indicating a conspiracy to conceal the handwriting.

2. That there was a great Elizabethan "plot" to conceal the authorship of the plays, because the plays were too revealing of intrigue and chicanery in the royal court. The Public must be led to believe they were written by that ignorant commoner from Stratford. This, of course, ignores the many plays that were non-political, and the utterly non-political poems that preceded the plays. This "plot," with many people in on it, continued from at least 1592 till at least 1640, but no hint of it ever leaked out;

3. That the Stratford monument, praising him in words carved in stone as the great writer, was fraudulently erected when he died, to further the "plot" and deceive the public;

4. Shortly after his death the "First Folio," containing all of his plays, was brought out, and was brought out ostensibly by the last two survivors of the Stratford man's old acting company. But that was all done as a hoax to deceive the

public as to the true authorship, and his two surviving fellow actors were merely lying for pay;

5. That incidents of autobiography are involved. Occasionally some incident in the plays seems to parallel some event in the life of this or that pretender, thus "proving" that that pretender must have been the author.

III

"Let's Forget for A While the The Thing Called Evidence"

ONCE, when that great Chicago lawyer, Clarence Darrow, was defending an ex-chief of Chicago police accused of crookedness, he began his address to the jury with these words.

> "Let's forget for a while the thing called evidence that seems to have buried my poor client in a sort of sand pile. After all, you are not lawyers, thank Heaven." (See Ben Hecht's *Gaily, Gaily*.)

That is the request our anti-Stratfordian friends are making of us—"Let's forget for a while the thing called evidence." Faced as they are with documents of unquestioned authenticity, by eye-witnesses who expressly stated that Shakespeare of Stratford was the author, and having no documented evidence of their own, our anti-Stratfordian friends have no alternative but either to ask us to forget the evidence, or else abandon hope.

Even without the documented evidence, which overwhelms them, the anti-Stratfordian theories fall of their own weight on close examination.

For they ask us to believe that the Stratford man was a fraud who succeeded in fooling his fellow actors for more than twenty years. Actually, of course, had he been a fraud, he could not have fooled his fellow actors for so long as one rehearsal. Yet for over twenty years, through thirty-six plays, he kept up this deception, they would have us believe—yet all the while his actors clasped him to their bosoms, produced the plays as his, left him bequests in their wills, acted as trustee for him in one deal, and after his death published all of the plays in the famous *First Folio*, expressly stating that they were written by their "friend" and "fellow" actor William Shakespeare. No hint of jealousy escaped from any of his fellow actors, and above all others they were the ones who knew.

Our anti-Stratfordian friends give us theories to answer this, but the theories collapse of their own weight.

Calvin Hoffman, "discoverer" of Christopher Marlowe, advances a theory of his own. Christopher Marlowe, his choice as pretender, had ostensibly been murdered in 1593, before the name "William Shakespeare" had publicly emerged; but Mr. Hoffman's theory is that Marlowe's "murder" was all a hoax and that in reality he had been secretly shipped off to Europe by his friend, Thomas Walsingham. In Europe, so Mr. Hoffman's theory runs, Marlowe wrote the Shakespearean plays one by one and sent them back to Thomas Walsingham for production on the London stage as "William Shakespeare's." Why Marlowe chose to say they were "William Shakespeare's" instead of merely writing under some made-up *nom-de-plume* Mr. Hoffman passes swiftly over. Instead of taking that simple course Thomas Walsingham, says Mr. Hoffman's theory, went to the London theatres, found the actor named William Shakespeare, and for pay induced him to foist off the plays onto his fellow actors as his own. But let Mr. Hoffman speak for himself, which he does as follows (*The Murder of the Man Who Was Shakespeare*, Universal Library Edition, Ch. 9, pp. 102-103):

> "He" (i.e., Walsingham) "would go to the London playhouses, and seek out some obscure actor, who would, for ample remuneration, lend his name to any work Walsingham would bring him.

"I believe that Walsingham went to London's theatres. That he found the actor he wanted; a steady, not too imaginative fellow, who could be trusted with his limited part in the enterprise and did not mind lending his name to anything as long as Walsingham's gold flowed freely.

"Walsingham found this man; a man with a family; a man who could conceivably be fostered as a playwright: William Shakespeare."

Odd that Walsingham saw fit to do it via William Shakespeare the actor, instead of merely adopting the simple course of a made-up *nom-de-plume*. But the toughest part is to tell us how William Shakespeare the actor fooled all of his fellow actors for so long and through thirty-six plays. For twenty years, while the name "William Shakespeare" became famous in literary and theatrical London, they held him to their bosom—with never a whisper of jealousy, or even comment. Isn't that expecting a bit too much of actors?

Mr. Looney, who "discovered" the Earl of Oxford as his pretender, advances a different theory of explanation.

First, as they all do, Looney dismissed the Stratford man's authorship as both "impossible" and "incredible"—then offered his theory.

His theory, all set forth in his *"Shakespeare" Identified*, was that the Stratford man didn't work all those years with his so-called "fellow" actors. Instead, having arrived in London from Stratford by 1592 he hit the jack pot in some unexplained way and in 1597 retired permanently to Stratford as a wealthy man and stayed there, never thereafter mingling with his "fellow" actors again. This, says Looney, got him out of London and kept him safely hidden in Stratford for all those vital years after 1597, leaving the field clear for the Earl of Oxford, as he wrote the plays, to have them produced in London as "William Shakespeare's."

Why Oxford wanted the plays produced as "William Shakespeare s," and not as his own, especially the non-political ones such as *Romeo & Juliet, Midsummer Night's Dream* and others to which Queen Elizabeth could have had no possible objection had Oxford's authorship been known, Looney fails to tell us satisfactorily. However, it is enough for the moment to point out that once more this theory asks us to forget for awhile the documented evidence. For, as document after document, all of unquestioned authenticity, reveal, it is simply not true that Shakespeare retired from London in 1597. He remained in London, busily active there with his fellow actors, till at least 1608—which was four years after the Earl of Oxford had died.

* * *

Thus we see that, even without reference to a large part of the affirmative documentary evidence, the basic theories of our anti-Stratfordian friends collapse of their own weight.

It is not, however, the collapse of their theories that gives us the incontrovertible story of the authorship. That story lies in the authentically documented records of the Shakespearean era.

IV

The Early Documented Proof That Shakespeare of Stratford Was the Author

IT STARTED early in his career, documented proof of his authorship, and mounted to an overwhelming climax at the end. Much of this evidence, though by no means all of it, is of fairly recent discovery.

On the facts known about the Stratford man in the 1850s, when anti-Stratfordianism really got under way, the claims of our anti-Stratfordian friends might conceivably have been tenable, at least arguably so, for so little was then known.

His Stratford monument was then known, on which his contemporaries had carved in stone the statement that he it was who was the writer; and the *First Folio* was then known, in which several contemporary witnesses had specifically stated that Shakespeare of Stratford was the playwright. But these, though in and of themselves overwhelming proof, seemed but the bare bones of proof and struck the swelling group of anti-Stratfordians as vulnerable. However, much flesh and blood has been added to those bare bones since.

For time has moved on since the 1850s, time and highly competent professional research—and our anti-Stratfordian friends have not moved with it. They continue today, very largely, to write and argue as though the situation were the same as in 1850. It is a cliché among them, stated time and again without further investigation, that "all the known facts of the Stratford man's life can be put on less than one page." Possibly in 1850 that was true, but not in 1964, as his four hundredth anniversary is celebrated.

In his *The Shakespeare Claimants* Mr. H. N. Gibson puts it this way, on p. 17:

> "As a matter of fact a considerable amount is now known about Shakespeare, and many former difficulties have been cleared up, but nearly all the discoveries have been made in recent years. They were not known when the search for Shakespearean substitutes began, and most of them have been published in works seldom perused by the general reader . . ."

As we seek, and wish to know, the incontrovertible story of the authorship, surmises and conjectures wholly untainted with evidentiary support must play no part. They can be, and repeatedly are, dreamt up out of totally whole cloth by nimble imaginations that have thrown off all restraint and discipline; and when, as time and again they do, they appear in the writings of our anti-Stratfordian friends, they sometimes read impressively to the uninformed. But that is not where the incontrovertible story is to be found.

It is to be found, has long been found, in the field where only true scholarship counts and where, ultimately, nothing is acceptable as evidence except documents of unquestioned authenticity.

The search for such documented evidence, with increasing acceleration in the past hundred years, has led straight through the records of the Elizabethan era, the millions of papers in the record offices of London and Stratford. There the lawsuits of the era are recorded, with original documents or certified copies, plus the sworn testimony of living eye-witnesses (once even the sworn written testimony of William Shakespeare himself). Those witnesses, then intent on the matter then being litigated, have revealed facts and presented papers that, at times, have thrown great light on Shakespeare's life. There, too, the wills of Shakespeare and his contemporaries are probated, and these, under the painstaking research of greatly gifted scholars have yielded up invaluable secrets. Also in those offices, in masses of dusty papers, usually poorly indexed, other authentically recorded facts of his day have lain waiting till ferreted out by dedicated scholarship.

It is from such sources that the evidence has come, the documented evidence, which our anti-Stratfordian friends would have us "forget for awhile"—would, in fact, have us cast entirely aside in order to dream with them in Anti-Stratfordia.

Documented proof that he was the author of the plays could not, of course, exist before the plays were written. They began to be written in the late 1580s or early 1590s; no one can fix a precise date. By 1598 documented evidence that he was the playwright began to appear.

But as early as 1593, which was almost thirty years before his contemporaries had told us in words carved in stone on his Stratford monument that he it was who was the great writer, and a full thirty years before several eye witnesses had told us in the *First Folio* that he it was who was the great playwright, evidence, clear and incontrovertible evidence, began to appear proving that William Shakespeare of Stratford was "William Shakespeare" the great poet, as distinguished from playwright. From that it necessarily followed that he was the great playwright as well; for Shakespeare, the author of the early poems *Venus & Adonis* and *The Rape of Lucrece*, was also Shakespeare, the author of the plays. That point to one ever has questioned, or possibly could.

Accordingly, the documented proof that Shakespeare of Stratford was "William Shakespeare," the great author, began in the year 1593.

A.

1593 — The Earliest Documented
Proof of His Authorship Appears

By 1592 Shakespeare was in London and had been there, working in the theatre, long enough to make his presence felt.

This we know from the book *Groatsworth of Wit,* written by the contemporary playwright Robert Greene and published in 1592. In it is Greene's well-known reference to him as the "upstart Crow" who was conceited enough to think he could both act and write the plays too, a "Johannes Factotum," and "the only Shake-scene in a country."

Greene, apparently, had found the young Shakespeare hard to take.

It was in the following year, 1593, that his *Venus & Adonis* was published, the first work ever to be published bearing the name "William Shakespeare" as author. That it was written by Shakespeare of Stratford and not by one of the pretenders is completely clear.

The book itself stated that it was written by William Shakespeare. If Oxford (or Bacon) wrote it, why did he say William Shakespeare wrote it? Our anti-Stratfordian friends attempt to explain this by telling us that Queen Elizabeth had clamped an injunction on Oxford (or Bacon), for political reasons, forbidding him to write under his own name.

In the first place, there is not one scintilla of evidence that Queen Elizabeth did any such thing. It is pure conjecture, wholly unsupported. And in the second place, if Queen Elizabeth did issue such an injunction it could have applied only to items having a political tinge, such as the killing of kings and the like—and there is nothing even faintly political about *Venus & Adonis.* It is sheer lyric poetry.

And remember, in signing the name William Shakespeare no precedent was being followed. This was the very first time the name had ever appeared in print as an author.

On the title page of the book the name was spelled in hyphenated form "William Shake-speare," and our anti-Stratfordian friends claim that this hyphenated spelling shows that the name was a *nom-de-plume*. That argument is pointless for two reasons. For the book contains the author's dedication to the Earl of Southampton, and the dedication is signed "William Shakespeare" without hyphenation. If the hyphenation revealed a *nom-de-plume*, it would have appeared in hyphenated form each time. Furthermore, occasional hyphenation of the name appears in several Shakespearean works, and in one of the dedicatory poems in the *First Folio*, and also in Ben Jonson's *Works*, it appears in both hyphenated and unhyphenated form in the same poem or article. The hyphenation obviously proves nothing.

Also, the pretenders, certainly the three most prominent of them, Bacon, Oxford and Marlowe, had written numerous works, never using this name as a *nom-de-plume*. Why, on this innocent lyric poem would any one of them suddenly have begun using as a *nom-de-plume* the full name of the actor from Stratford—not only his last name "Shakespeare" but also his first name "William?" Our anti-Stratfordian friends pass hurriedly over that point.

Furthermore, the publisher of the book *Venus & Adonis* was Richard Field, a fact that becomes most significant when we realize that Richard Field grew up in Stratford from boyhood as William Shakespeare's neighbor. When Richard Field's father died it was William Shakespeare's father who was called in to appraise his estate. At the age of fifteen Richard Field had been sent from Stratford to London by his father and apprenticed to Thomas Vautrollier, a prominent book-publisher. In ten years Vautrollier had died, Richard Field had married the

21

widow and owned the business. Thus is was that in 1593, when Shakespeare was twenty-nine and Richard Field thirty-one, Field was one of twenty-two master printers licensed to operate in London. Naturally enough, when Shakespeare wanted his first book *Venus & Adonis,* published, it was to the Stratford boy, Richard Field, that he turned.

But the truly crushing feature of *Venus & Adonis* is its famous dedication to the Earl of Southampton. This could have been written by no one but the man whose name is signed to it. It read as follows:

> "To the Right Honourable Henry Wriothesly, Earl of Southampton and Baron of Tichfield:
>
> Right Honourable:
>
> I know not how I shall offend in dedicating my unpolished lines to your lordship, nor how the world will censure me for choosing so strong a prop to support so weak a burden; only if your honour seem but pleased, I account myself highly praised, and vow to take advantage of all idle hours, till I have honoured you with some graver labor. But if the first heir of my invention prove deformed, I shall be sorry it had so noble a godfather, and never after ear so barren a land, for fear it yield me still so bad a harvest. I leave it to your honourable survey, and your honour to your heart's content, which I wish may always answer your own wish and the world's hopeful expectation.
>
> Your honour's in all duty,
> William Shakespeare."

In 1593, when that dedication was published, the Earl of Oxford was forty-three years old, the Seventeenth Earl in direct succession, probably the number one peer of England outside the royal family, and demonstrably a favourite of the Queen herself. Southampton was then in his late teens, apparently a beautiful youth but far beneath Oxford in rank, being but the third Earl in direct succession. Would Oxford conceivably have demeaned himself by writing that sycophantish dedication to him? Our anti-Stratfordian friends have been known to say that Oxford loved Southampton because Oxford was (they say) really Southampton's father. But that is impossible, because at one point Southampton's mother negotiated for awhile to arrange a marriage between Southampton and Oxford's daughter. (See Rowse, *William Shakespeare*, pp. 139 et seq.)

Nor would Bacon, England's greatest lawyer, or the wildly rebellious Marlowe, have written such a dedication. It is wholly inconceivable.

Next, true to the promise made in that first dedication, Shakespeare proceeded to "take advantage of all idle hours" and to produce in the very next year, 1594, that "graver labor" he had said he would, namely, his poem *The Rape of Lucrece*. Again it was Richard Field who did the printing and again it was dedicated to the young Earl of Southampton—and this time, if that were possible, the dedication is even more devastating to the pretenders than was that in *Venus & Adonis*. Again it should be read in full. It was as follows:

> "To the Right Honourable Henry Wriothesly, Earl of Southampton and Baron of Tichfield:
>
> The love I dedicate to your lordship is without end; whereof this pamphlet, without beginning, is but a superfluous moiety. The warrant I have of your honourable disposition, not the worth of my untutored lines, makes it assured of acceptance. What I have done is yours; what I have to do is yours; being part in all I have, devoted yours. Were my worth greater, my duty would show greater; meantime, as it is, it is bound to your lordship, to whom I wish long life, still lengthened with all happiness.
>
> William Shakespeare."

Convinced as they are that it is *"impossible* that that *Stratford* man was the author," our anti-Stratfordian friends ask us to accept, in lieu of this solidly documented evidence, their wholly unsupported theory that one of the pretenders wrote these dedications. Thus they ask us, with no evidence to support them, to believe that the erudite Bacon, England's greatest lawyer and himself with many works already published, referred in the first instance to the poem as "my unpolished lines" and in the second instance as "my untutored lines." Oxford too had had the finest of English educations and had already written much charming poetry which he had circulated in manuscript among the nobility; yet, they ask us to believe, he not only referred to the poem as "my untutored lines" but also as "the first heire of my invention." The same applies to Marlowe.

Would those proud and eminent Elizabethans have prostrated themselves before the teen-age Southampton with the words "were my worth greater?" Or have commented in those dedications on how they might "offend" the young Southampton by dedicating the poems to him? Or expressed concern about how "the world will censure" them for doing so? Or have stated that if Southampton were offended they would never write again? It does indeed strain credulity far past the breaking point to say so.

Those dedications could have been written by only one man of the era, namely the "upstart Crow" from Stratford, eager to get ahead in Elizabethan London in the only way open to him.

B.

"For My Name Is Will"

Fortunately, as we seek the incontrovertible proof of authorship, we have a priceless witness in William Shakespeare himself. For in one of the Sonnets the author categorically informs us that his name was "Will"—a name which no one but the man from Stratford had.

It came in Sonnet 136, one of the Sonnets addressed to the famous or infamous Dark Lady, the woman who for awhile so clearly held the author in helpless infatuation.

It begins with these words:

> "If thy soul check thee that I come so near,
> Swear to thy blind soul that I was thy 'Will,' "

Then, as its final couplet, he comes right out with these all-revealing words:

> "Make but my name thy love, and love that still,
> And then thou lovest me, for my name is 'Will.' "

Since the Sonnets, when eventually published in 1609, expressly stated that they were written by William Shakespeare, and since in the above Sonnet 136 the author expressly stated that "my name is Will," it does indeed seem impossible for any pretender to stand up in front of it. Wise it is on their part for practically every one of our anti-Stratfordian friends to treat this Sonnet as they usually do—i.e., totally to ignore it.

However, one or two have stood up and attempted to fight back.

Not one of the many pretenders was named "Will," nor is there one scintilla of evidence that any one of them was ever called "Will." However, the backers of the Seventeenth Earl of Oxford's pretendership (Oxford's only given name having been Edward) have made a pass at trying to explain Sonnet 136 away.

Says Looney, discoverer of Oxford as the true Shakespeare, in his *"Shakespeare" Identified,* p. 292:

> "The two enigmatical sonnets in which he plays upon the word 'will' finish with the striking and emphatic sentence
> 'for my name is Will.'

"Had those words been written by a man whose real name

25

was William, like the Stratford man, they would have been as puerile as anything in English literature."

"Puerile?" A Shakespearean sonnet? Doth he not protest too much? He actually argues that because the author said "my name is Will," his name could *not* have been "William."

In their *Shakespeare, The Real Man Behind The Name*, the Ogburns also attempt to explain this matter away. On page 82 they say:

> "Both he" (i.e., Oxford) "and the young man" (i.e., the author's intimate friend) "were known as 'Will', as is seen in some of the Sonnets addressed to the Dark Lady, for instance number 135..."

Thus, to prove that Oxford was known as "Will" they cite the Sonnets which state that the author's name was "Will." This does seem to be a case of using their own theory that Oxford was the author as a fact to prove that Oxford was the author.

C.

1598 — The Earliest Documented Proof of His Authorship of the Plays Appears

Prior to 1598 a few of the plays got published, no one knows on whose authority or who gave the scripts to the printer, but in each instance without the author's name. These included *King John, Titus Andronicus, Taming of the Shrew, Richard Second, Richard Third, Romeo and Juliet,* and at least part of *Henry VI* (*Chambers,* Vol. 1, pp. 275 et seq.).

Beginning in 1598, however, as publication of the plays continued (with the authorization still unknown), it was almost always with his name stated as author, though in one or two instances no name was given.

Thus in 1598 appeared Quarto 2 of *The Tragedie of King Richard the Third* "By William Shake-speare;" Quarto 1, *Love's Labour's Lost* "newly corrected and augmented by W. Shakespeare;" and Quarto 2 of *The Tragedie of King Richard the Second* "By William Shake-speare." *(Chambers,* Vol. I, pp. 294 et seq.*)*. As other publications came out in the years that followed, his name as author was sometimes spelled in hyphenated form, sometimes in non-hyphenated form.

Also in 1598 one Francis Meres published in London his book *Palladis Tamia* (meaning Pallas' Housekeeper).

Meres was a minister and a school teacher of the Elizabethan era, and Sir Edmund Chambers says this of him in his great book *William Shakespeare* (Vol. II, p. 193, herein referred to as Chambers):

> "He was living in London in 1597 and 1598, and seems to have been in touch with literary men. From 1602 he was rector and schoolmaster at Wing, Rutland."

In his *Palladis Tamia* Meres reviewed London's literary scene in 1598, considering first England's eminent poets and then her eminent playwrights. Of the poets he said.

> "The English tongue is mightily enriched, and gorgeously invested in rare ornaments and splendid abiliments by sir *Philip Sidney, Spencer, Daniel, Drayton, Warner, Shakespeare, Marlow* and *Chapman*", adding that ". . . the sweete wittie soule of Ovid lives in mellifluous and honey-tongued Shakespeare . . ."

Next, leaving poetry, he took up drama, and said:

> "As *Plautus* and *Seneca* are accounted the best in Comedy and Tragedy among the Latines, so *Shakespeare* among the English is the most excellent in both kinds for the stage."

With that he did for Shakespeare what he did for no other

27

author whom he mentions, namely lists his then known works. He names eleven of the plays (omitting for some reason the three parts of *Henry VI* and *Taming of the Shrew*), and credits the authorship of every one of them to Shakespeare.

Having thus mentioned only Shakespeare as the best in both tragedy and comedy, he proceeds to give a long list of authors as "our best for Tragedie," naming thirteen, including Shakespeare, and follows it by naming seventeen as "the best for Comedy." In that seventeen he names both Shakespeare and the Earl of Oxford. From this we know that Oxford did write some comedies, none of which has survived. (For all quotes see *Chambers*, Vol. II, pp. 193 et seq.).

Thus we see the only literary historian of the day telling us not only of Shakespeare but also of two prominent pretenders, Oxford and Marlowe, and telling us of them as three separate men. Difficult indeed it is for our anti-Stratfordian friends to explain this away—but occasionally we do find anti-Stratfordian authors attempting to explain it.

They do this on their theory (wholly without evidentiary support) that a great Elizabethan "plot" existed to hide the true authorship; and Meres, they insist, must have been in on it. In other words, Meres, schoolmaster and rector, must have been lying for pay.

Thus, in its issue of September, 1959, p. 994, the *American Bar Association Journal* tells us categorically:

> "In 1598 Meres was commissioned to publicize the pseudonym in his *Palladis Tamia* . . . Meres mentions Shakespeare in various categories. In an early one he also mentions Oxford's name as a dramatist. It would have been too suspicious if he had left him out entirely . . ."

"Suspicious!" Plots, plots everywhere—but no evidence to prove them!

And in their *Shakespeare, The Real Man Behind The Name*

(p. 37), the Ogburns continue this unsupported theory of plot and suspicion with this attempt to explain Meres away:

"The inclusion of Oxford along with Shakespeare, taken by some to indicate he was a different person, is explicable on the grounds that he was too well known as a dramatist in his own right to be excluded—certainly without exciting suspicion."

Obviously it would never have done to excite suspicion. Someone might have guessed the whole "plot" and seen through the hoax. But no one ever did.

And as for Oxford being "too well known as a dramatist," the evidence of that is on the ephemeral side, consisting in the main of Meres' simple statement, above-quoted, that he and sixteen others were "among the best for comedy" and a no more informative statement by Puttenham in his "Art of English Poesie," in 1589. Not one of his comedies has survived.

True, when Meres mentions "Shakespeare" he does not expressly call him "Shakespeare of Stratford," and our anti-Stratfordian friends argue from that that he was not referring to Shakespeare of Stratford but to the great unknown "Shakespeare" who in reality was Oxford or Bacon or Marlowe.

But that is impossible, for in *Palladis Tamia* Meres tells us that in that year 1598 Shakespeare was circulating "his sugred sonnets among his private friends."

Since he thus knew that in 1598 Shakespeare was circulating "his sugred sonnets among his private friends," the Sonnets that were being circulated must have been circulated as "Shakespeare's." Otherwise how did Meres know that in 1598 "Shakepeare" was circulating them?

Not even by recourse to their "plot" theory can our anti-Stratfordian friends brush this bit of crushing documentary evidence aside.

It would have been impossible for Oxford to have signed these sonnets with a *nom-de-plume* "Shakespeare" and circulated them among *his* private friends, for that would have given the whole "plot" away. If they were, as Meres says they were, being circulated as "Shakespeare's," not one of the pretenders, be he Bacon, Oxford, Marlowe, or whoever, could possibly have had a hand in it, for had one of them done so then all those among whom they were being circulated would have instantly seen through the "hoax" as to the entire authorship. It could only have been Shakespeare himself who was thus circulating them.

Our anti-Stratfordian friends have never suggested an answer to that.

D.

"By The Dimme Light of Nature"

Next we may consider a priceless document of recent discovery, a letter written by Francis Beaumont to Ben Jonson in 1615, shortly before both Beaumont and Shakespeare died.

Beaumont was Shakespeare's contemporary playwright, of the "Beaumont and Fletcher" team; Ben Jonson was the contemporary playwright deemed, after Marlowe, as second only to Shakespeare in importance. Both Beaumont and Jonson could not have failed to know who the author of the Shakespearean works was, and in fact many scholars believe that each of them at times, collaborated with Shakespeare on certain plays.

The letter was first discovered around 1921, and was first printed in full in 1930 by Sir Edmund Chambers in his great book *(William Shakespeare,* Vol. II, pp. 222 et seq.), where its entire history is given. It is currently in the Pierpont Morgan Library in New York.

Beaumont was apparently in the country at the time, writing

to Ben Jonson in the city. He phrased his letter in verse, which seems to have been his custom when writing to Jonson, for, as Sir Edmund Chambers tells us, he "wrote another well-known verse epistle to Jonson," and he filled his letter with gossipy bits of commonplace news and criticisms. In it he refers to Shakespeare in words that are completely revealing.

Beaumont began the letter as follows:

"Neither to follow fashion nor to showe my witt ...
... wrote I this letter but to showe
The Love I carrie and mee thinkes do owe
To you ... "

He then goes on to add:

"... heere I would let slippe
(If I had any in mee) schollershippe,
And from all Learninge keepe these lines as cleere
As Shakespeares best are, which our heires shall heare
Preachers apte to their auditors to showe
How farr sometimes a mortall man may goe
By the dimme light of Nature ... "

Here we see one contemporary playwright writing to another contemporary playwright a personal letter, not for publication. Both of them, Beaumont and Jonson, knew their own contemporary playwright Shakespeare, whoever he was; and here, in simple language not intended either for the public eye or for posterity, one of them tells the other of the profound admiration he has for Shakespeare. And in telling him he refers to Shakespeare as having gone far without "schollershippe" but "by the dimme light of Nature."

By no stretch of the imagination can it be said that Beaumont was referring to Bacon, or Oxford, or Marlowe, all highly educated scholars. The words fit only the man from Stratford. The letter is a priceless document, written by a man who knew the

31

facts to another who also knew the facts. It is indeed a document that cannot be rationalized away.

Commenting on this letter Sir Edmund Chambers says (*Chambers*, Vol. I, p. 70):

> "And if Jonson smiled at Shakespeare's 'small Latine, and lesse Greeke,' his judgment chimes precisely with the reference, so full of admiration and discriminating kindliness, in the recently recovered lines of Francis Beaumont."

V

The Documents Showing Long and Intimate Association Between Shakespeare of Stratford and His Fellow Actors

THOUGH the documents we have just examined in the preceding chapter show clearly that Shakespeare of Stratford was the author, they are not wholly satisfying, because in not one of them does a qualified eye-witness explicitly state that it was the actor from Stratford who wrote the works.

Explicit statements that the Stratford man was the author came later, by eye-witnesses of unimpeachable stature and perfect qualification, largely via his Stratford monument and the *First Folio*. But before considering them it is important that first we review the documents that show who those eye-witnesses were and how long and intimate his association with them had been.

A.

The Chamberlain's Company LATER KING'S MEN

Two professional groups of actors dominated the London stage throughout Shakespeare's active life. One was known as the Chamberlain's Company, because it was under the patronage and protection of Lord Hunsdon, Elizabeth's closest living relative and Lord Chamberlain of her Court; the other was known as the Admiral's Company, because it was under the patronage and protection of Lord Howard of Effingham, Lord High Admiral of England.

It was to the Chamberlain's Company that William Shakespeare belonged throughout the entirety of his professional career; and from the late 1590s onward he was a substantial co-owner of it, all thoroughly documented, as we shall shortly see. Upon Elizabeth's death, James VI of Scotland ascended to the throne as James I of England, and immediately took the Chamberlain's Company under his own patronage, and from then onward it was known not as the Chamberlain's Company but as the King's Men. The personnel of its principal actors remained largely unchanged throughout Shakespeare's active life.

The earliest known document showing Shakespeare a member of the Chamberlain's Company is an official entry in the records of Privy Council showing payment on March 15, 1595, to "William Kempe, William Shakespeare & Richard Burbage, servantes to the Lord Chamberlayne", for plays presented at Court before the Queen in December, 1594. It is a document that has no bearing on the question of authorship but is of interest as the earliest of the many documents showing Shakespeare a Chamberlain's Company man.

B.

In 1598 Shakespeare and His Fellow
Actors Hi-Jack their "Theatre,"
Move It Across the Thames, and Re-christen it the "Globe"

It would be impossible for any single event to reveal more clearly how closely and intimately Shakespeare and his fellow

34

actors in the Chamberlain's Company worked together than is revealed by their illegal and thoroughly documented hi-jacking of the *Theatre*, moving it across the Thames, and re-christening it the *Globe*.

All of the documents were discovered in 1909 by Dr. C. W. Wallace and published by him in 1910 in his *Nebraska University Studies*. (See also *Chambers*, Vol. II, pages 52 et seq.)

It occurred in 1598 and early 1599, when William Shakespeare had reached a mature thirty-five years of age.

Till late in 1598, and for years prior to that, the Chamberlain's Company had been producing its plays in the *Theatre*, a playhouse built years before by James Burbage and on his death inherited by his two sons, Richard Burbage, star actor of the Chamberlain's Company, and Cuthbert, his brother, business manager.

But the *Theatre* had been erected on land belonging to someone else, one Giles Allen, under a ground-lease that ran for twenty-one years with an express provision that the Burbages could remove it "at any time or times" before the end of the twenty-one year term. But on April 13, 1597, that term expired —with no move by the Burbages to take advantage of the removal clause.

As any lawyer will instantly see, by failing to remove it within the term of the lease the Burbages automatically lost all title to it and all right to remove it, under both English and American law. From that moment on it belonged to the land-owner, Giles Allen—and he obviously knew it.

Many long negotiations had been held between the Burbages and Allen, looking towards a renewal of the ground-lease; and at one point a new lease had been drawn. But Allen, apparently playing cat-and-mouse, never signed the new lease and dragged the negotiations on beyond the dead line. The Burbages were two years behind in their rent, which may have influenced Allen's thinking a bit. In any event, feeling secure in his own

35

ownership of the building, Allen finally flatly refused either to renew or to discuss the matter further.

This must have given the actors of the Chamberlain's Company quite a shock. They suddenly saw that they had no theatre. In this pinch they all (William Shakespeare demonstrably included) revealed themselves as men of daring as well as talent. They decided to remove the building anyway.

They would, they decided, steal the building, set it up elsewhere, and claim it as their own—as true a hi-jacking operation as any that ever came out of the City of Chicago. And that was what they did—with William Shakespeare not only demonstrably a prime mover in the conspiracy, but, as one document shows, probably even master-minding it.

First, of course, they must acquire land for the new location— and with considerable surreptitiousness they set about doing so. A desirable plot in Southwark, across the river Thames, was located. It belonged to one Nicholas Brend, or to his father, and proved happily available. On Christmas Day, 1598, the conspiring actors leased it from him for thirty-one years, at a rental of just over fourteen pounds per year.

That lease was the first, and very essential, overt act in the criminal conspiracy they were now cooking up. It was signed by seven members of the Chamberlain's Company, namely Richard Burbage, Cuthbert Burbage, William Shakespeare, John Heminges, Augustine Phillips, Thomas Pope and William Kempe. The original lease has as yet never been found, but a certified transcript from it was filed in a lawsuit in 1616 between John Heminges and his daughter Thomasine Ostler concerning shares in the *Globe* (*Ostler v. Heminges,* Coram Rege Roll, 1454), where it was discovered in 1909 by Dr. C. W. Wallace. (See *The Globe Playhouse,* by John Cranford Adams, p. 12.)

Having thus lined up their ground space, all was in readiness. Nothing remained but to wait for an advantageous moment when Giles Allen was not looking, hastily dismantle the building and rush it across the river—all in true gangster style. Elizabethan virtuosity, surely, but not without a certain modern tinge as well.

They did not have to wait long. On December 28, 1598, just three days after they had completed negotiations for the lease of their new ground, Giles Allen relaxed his guard and went down to his country place in Essex. Obviously the actors were watching him, for on that very day they showed up at the *Theatre* (William Shakespeare not being recorded as either present or absent) with a dismantling crew and an experienced London carpenter, Peter Streete, and with the Burbages' mother coming along with loud voicings of thorough approval. The old lady, as many documents over the years prove, was definitely a fighter. In all, they numbered twelve.

Apparently Giles Allen had suspected that this might happen, for he had left not one but two guards to protect his building. They must have been trusting souls, however, for they were lulled into complete non-interference when Cuthbert Burbage and Peter Streete told them they were merely taking the building down to replace it at the same site after repairing certain decayed spots.

There being no telephones, Giles Allen remained unaware of all this as he relaxed on his country estate, and the conspirators had three days for uninterrupted work. These they took full advantage of.

Under the expert eye of Peter Streete they quickly dismantled the *Theatre*, rushed its timbers to Streete's own wharf on the Thames, and thence ferried them across the river to the new site in Southwark. There, with some additions (estimated at four hundred pounds' worth by Dr. Adams, *The Globe Playhouse*,

p. 18), it was reassembled and given a new name, the *Globe*. Thus it was that the *Globe* playhouse, immortal as the theatre in which for many years Shakespeare's plays were produced, came into being.

This high-handed proceeding, of course, resulted in prompt litigation, where all the facts were aired and recorded for history. Giles Allen promptly brought suit in trespass against the Burbages and Peter Streete in the Court of Queen's Bench, claiming eight hundred pounds damages. A more thorough lawyer would no doubt have joined all the conspirators as parties defendant, but Allen's lawyer did not. Nor did he resort to criminal prosecution. Peter Streete landed temporarily in jail, but beyond that no resort to criminal prosecution was taken.

Surprising to report, Giles Allen did not win. Cuthbert Burbage promptly sued Allen in the Court of Requests and induced that court not only to enjoin Allen's Queen's Bench action but eventually to give judgment for Burbage on the ground that Allen had been deceitful in dragging out the lease-renewal conferences. Allen thereupon brought a new suit in Queen's Bench, and followed it with a suit in Star Chamber, in the latter of which he claimed that Burbage had won the earlier suit in the Court of Requests by intimidating Allen's witnesses, by perjury and subornation of perjury, and by forgery of a court record. He was sensational, but he lost—and was never paid a shilling. All of the court documents are printed in full in Dr. Wallace's *The First London Theatre*, Vol. XIII, *University Studies*, University of Nebraska. (See also *Chambers*, Vol. II, pp. 52 et seq.)

The role of leadership which William Shakespeare played in this hi-jacking episode seems clearly revealed from the records of the lawyer for the landlord on whose land the *Globe* was erected. For in May, 1599, five months after the hi-jacking coup, that landlord, Brend, died, and in listing the assets of his estate his lawyer described the *Globe*, in Latin, as "a building of late

erected in the occupation of William Shakespeare and others."
In his *A Life of William Shakespeare,* p. 287, Mr. J. Quincy
Adams quotes from the documentation of this as follows:

> "On May 16, 1599, a post-mortem inquisition of the estate
> of Sir Thomas Brend, father of Sir Nicholas, was taken. Among
> his other properties in Southwark was listed the *Globe* play-
> house, described as "una domo de nova edificata . . . in occupa-
> cione Willelmi Shakespeare et aliorum."

In that lawyer's eye, at any rate, the leader of that little group
of conspirators was clearly William Shakespeare.

In this joint and almost surely criminal venture, which fortunately turned out so happily, we have clearly revealed for us
the trust and confidence these actors felt for one another, and the
intimacy in which they worked as they carried on together their
theatre life.

C.

Shakespeare Becomes A Co-Owner of His Company's Theaters

As a direct outgrowth of the hi-jacking coup, and apparently
as part of the deal, Shakespeare became a part owner of the
Globe.

The transportation of the *Theatre* across the Thames, and the
setting of it up as the *Globe* with four hundred pounds of new or
replacement additions, required an amount of capital quite substantial for those days. To raise it the Burbages turned to their
fellow actors and co-conspirators, including William Shakespeare. As Cuthbert Burbage put it in his *Answer* filed to a *Petition* to the Lord Chamberlain in 1635, he and his brother Richard "joyned those deserving men, Shakspere, Hemings, Con-

dell, Philips and others as partners in the profits." *(Chambers,* Vol. II, p. 66.)

The percentages of interest each actor acquired are all documentarily revealed in the litigations that their heirs brought to settle questions as to who owned what shares. Some of these litigations were discovered by Professor C. W. Wallace in 1909, some earlier. All of the relevant portions of the documents are printed in Sir Edmund Chambers' book *(Chambers,* Vol. II, pp 52 et seq.).

The Burbages retained a one-half interest in the *Globe,* and the remaining one-half was divided equally among the five other conspirators, William Shakespeare, John Hemings, Augustine Phillips, Thomas Pope and William Kempe, making Shakespeare initially a one-tenth owner.

That was in 1599. Later, in 1608, his Company (which by then had changed its name from the Chamberlain's Company to the King's Men) was to acquire the Blackfriars theatre, and upon their doing so, as the above documents also show, Shakespeare became a one-seventh owner of it, the other six being the two Burbages, John Heminges, Henry Condell, William Sly and William Ostler.

As other shareholders died or sold their shares Shakespeare's interests fluctuated to some extent. As Sir Edmund Chambers puts it *(Chambers,* Vol. II, p. 67):

"Whether he held his shares to the end of his life, and if not, when he parted with them, is not clear. They are not mentioned specifically in his will, although the residuary bequests of 'leases' to the Halls would cover them . . ."

Thus we see how more and more closely the actors of this Company, including Shakespeare, were joined to each other in their theatrical venture, which was also their life.

D.

The Actors of the Chamberlain's Company,
Including William Shakespeare, Become "His
Majesty's Grooms of the Chamber" Under
King James, Following Elizabeth's Death.

On March 24, 1603, Queen Elizabeth died, and on May 7 her distant relative, James the Sixth of Scotland, arrived in London to assume the throne as James the First of England. Once more Fortune smiled, not only on the actors but on posterity as well, for James, like Elizabeth, loved the theatre—and Shakespeare continued to thrive.

On May 17, 1603, just ten days after his arrival in London, James issued royal letters patent to actors of the Chamberlain's Company, licensing them to continue producing plays, not merely for the general public but for the King's own "solace and pleasure" as well. From that time on the Chamberlain's Company was known as the "King's Men."

In the letters patent the actors were individually named. Heading the list was Lawrence Fletcher, a newcomer whom James had brought down from Scotland with him. The second name in the list was "William Shakespeare," revealing his importance. Richard Burbage came third, followed by Augustine Phillips, John Heminges, Henry Condell, William Sly, Richard Cowley and Robert Arnim, in that order. *(Chambers,* Vol. II, p. 72.)

Things got off to a bad start, for soon the plague was raging in London and when James was crowned on July 25 the public was not admitted. All theatres were closed, the actors went on tour and the King himself eventually got out of town. In November he summoned them to play for him in the country, which they did for the first time on December 2, 1603.

But by March, 1604, the plague was gone and the King's postponed triumphal procession was put on. The actors were invited to take part in the parade, and to make sure they were properly dressed for the royal occasion an official document was issued listing the actors by name to whom scarlet cloth was to be issued. The name "William Shakespeare" headed the list, with Lawrence Fletcher demoted to third. (*Chambers,* Vol. II, p. 73.)

Then, in August, 1604, the Envoy from Spain arrived to negotiate a treaty of peace, and Somerset House, the finest palace in London, was turned over to him. He did not speak English, hence no play could be put on for him, but the King nevertheless sent the entire group of his favorite actors to entertain the Envoy with their continued presence. From August 9 to August 27, 1604, twelve members of the King's Men, officially referred to as "His Majesty's Grooms of the Chamber and players," stayed in Somerset House, adding their talents to the gaiety of the occasion. It was a high honor, but in addition the King rewarded them financially. Twenty pounds were paid to John Heminges and Augustine Phillips "for the allowance of themselves and ten of their fellows, his Majesty's Grooms of the Chamber and players, for waiting and attending on his Majesty's service, by commandment, upon the Spanish Ambassador at Somerset House, for the space of eighteen days."

No document expressly states that William Shakespeare was there, but since the twenty pounds was for Augustine Phillips, John Heminges, "and ten of their fellows," and since that number of twelve covers the principal actors in the King's Men (and for such a rare and magnificent outing every man unquestionably "pulled his rank" to get to go), it is quite certain that Shakespeare was there.

E.

He Inherits Under the Will of His Fellow Actor, Augustine Phillips

In 1605 Augustine Phillips, long a member of the Chamberlain's Company—King's Men group, died, and in his will left thirty shillings in gold to his "fellow" actor "William Shakespeare."

For some reason the Ogburns, *American Bar Association Journal* authors, in their subsequent book *Shakespeare, The Real Man Behind the Name* (p. 112), erroneously state that Augustine Phillips' will "does not identify him as an actor but simply lists him as among 'the hired men' of the company."

The will is printed by Edmund Chambers *(Chambers,* Vol. II, pp. 73-74), and in very clear and explicit language first leaves five pounds "unto and amongst the hyred men of the Company," to be equally distributed among them, and them provides:

> "I geve and bequeathe to my Fellowe William Shakespeare a thirty shillings peece in Gould, To My Fellowe Henry Condell one other thirty shillings peece in gould"

and then makes twenty-shilling bequests to five others of his fellow actors.

Thus not only did Augustine Phillips leave him a bequest as his "Fellowe" actor, he also mentioned "William Shakespeare" first of all—and left him the largest bequest of all except for the one of equal size to Condell.

Again we see the long and affectionate intimacy between William Shakespeare and his fellow actors.

F.

He Continues as One of the "Men Players" Till at Least 1608

This is documented for us by Cuthbert Burbage himself. In his *Answer* to a *Petition* to the Lord Chamberlain, in 1635, he tells how he and his brother Richard in 1608 purchased the lease of the Blackfriars theatre "with our money" and then "placed men Players, which were Heminges, Condell, Shakspeare, etc" in as co-partners with them (*Chambers*, Vol. II, p. 66).

G.

He Is Retained, Along With His Fellow Actor Richard Burbage, To Make An "Impressa" For The Earl of Rutland

March 24, 1613, being an anniversary of King James' ascension to the throne, a so-called "tournament" was held to celebrate the occasion, and the various knights carried shields or "imprese" made of canvas which contained two items, one a picture and the other a motto. The two items were supposed to give a clue to the knight's identity, and a courtly guessing game followed, as to who each knight was.

All of the knights strove to outdo each other in cleverness. Clever enough to know he needed help was the Earl of Rutland —and with great astuteness he sought it from that vastly talented pair, William Shakespeare and his fellow actor Richard Burbage. Together they dreamt-up an "impresa" for him, clever motto and clever picture too, for which each was paid forty three shillings in gold. This is documented by the following entry in the accounts of the 6th Earl of Rutland, dated March 31, 1613 *(Chambers,* Vol. II, p. 153):

> "Item, 31 Martii, to Mr. Shakspeare in gold about my Lorde's impreso, xliiij[s]; to Richard Burbage for yaynting and making yt, in gold xliiij[s]."

The American Bar Association Journal, February, 1959, p. 145, refers to this as "a doubtful record," but that greatest of Elizabethan scholars, Sir Edmund Chambers, says *(Chambers,* Vol. II, p. 153):

> "There is no reason to doubt that the payment was to the poet, as the association with Burbage, known to have been a painter, suggests."

VI

His Will Throws Great and Revealing Light on the Question of Authorship

TWO items in his will are of the very greatest importance, as we seek the incontrovertible story of the authorship, namely, his appointment of Thomas Russell as his testamentary "overseer," and his bequests to the then surviving three of his old fellow actors.

A.

He Appoints Thomas Russell, Nobleman of Stratford, His Testamentary "Overseer"

In his will Shakespeare did "intreat and appoint" Thomas Russell, "Esquier," and Francis Collins "to be overseers hereof."

Francis Collins was the Stratford attorney who drew the will. The identity of Thomas Russell was not pinpointed until 1937.

The position of "overseer" of a will is one no longer encountered today; but in the 1600s the "custom of appointing overseers or supervisors was universal among persons of any social standing in Elizabethan England." (Hotson, *I, William Shakespeare*, p. 13.) It was the executor's duty to carry out the provisions of the will; it was the overseer's duty to see that he did so.

It was in 1937 that Dr. Leslie Hotson identified this Thomas Russell, and, with his usual impeccable documentation, gave us the full story in his *I, William Shakespeare*.

Thomas Russell was the second son of Sir Thomas Russell, the Lord of Strensham Castle, a few miles down the Avon from Stratford. To the west of Strensham Castle stretched Malvern Chase, where in Shakespeare's youth the elder Thomas Russell ruled as "Forester and Master of the Game." The Castle itself had been built in the fourteenth century by the then Sir John Russell (unfortunately for him a favorite of Richard II), and was fated to be destroyed in the 1640s by Oliver Cromwell's revolutionaries—but that came a quarter of a century after Shakespeare's death.

It was in 1570 that this younger son, and namesake, of Sir Thomas Russell was born, making him six years William Shakespeare's junior. He was baptized in Strensham Church, "among the monuments and escutcheons of his ancestors," better born than was Elizabeth's Lord Chancellor, Hatton, or Cecil, her greatest minister.

Thus highly born, this Thomas Russell all his life was demonstrably intimate with and closely associated with the top society of the Elizabethan era.

Upon the father's death, this second son, "Thomas", inherited in the father's will two manors, both near Stratford. One of these was "Alderminster," on Stratford's very outskirts, and it was his manor "Alderminster" that in Shakespeare's day Thomas Russell established as his home. There he lived with his second wife, widow of the well-known scientist Thomas Digges, and there he raised his stepson Leonard Digges, whom he brought to live in "Alderminster" in 1600, when Leonard was twelve years old.

Since Leonard Digges later, in the *First Folio,* gives us his own unimpeachable testimony that Shakespeare of Stratford was the author, it is the light which Thomas Russell's appointmen throws on Leonard, the young step-son, that is the most important feature of the appointment. For since Shakespeare was on such intimate terms with Thomas Russell the stepfather as to appoint him in 1616 his testamentary "overseer," he could not fail to have been at least *known* in "Alderminster," the Russell home; nor could the young step-son Leonard, living there since 1600, when he was twelve, and himself to mature into a man of poetic talent, have failed at least to know who Shakespeare of Stratford was. And in the *First Folio* he tells us.

Also, at "Alderminster" all the experience of daily lordly living was available for Shakespeare to see and observe, possibly for himself to experience. And certainly, through Thomas Russell, any door in England could have been opened for him, including Southampton's and Francis Bacon's.

All of this is impeccably documented in Leslie Hotson's *I, William Shakespeare,* published in 1937.

B.

He Leaves Bequests To the Three Surviving Members of His Old Fellow Actors

It was in April, 1616, that Shakespeare died. In January of that year his then Stratford lawyer, Francis Collins, drew up a draft of his will. Certain lines in that draft were scratched out and certain additions were made by interlineation; and in that scratched-up form it was executed in March, some seven weeks before he died, and later in that form probated. *(Chambers,* Vol. II, pp. 169 et seq.)

To his wife, by interlineation between the lines of the will's original draft, he left his "second best bed", thereby touching off centuries of speculation as to whether this was intended as a slight or not. In any event, Anne was already well provided for by her dower rights.

He also, and this is the will's second important feature, left the famous bequests of small sums "to my fellowes John Hemynge, Richard Burbage and Henry Cundell . . . to buy them Ringes." Those three, Heminges, Burbage and Condell, were the last of his old fellow actors then still alive.

These bequests are of great importance, because they are one of several pieces of documentary evidence that show William Shakespeare of Stratford as having been the William Shakespeare who was a fellow actor with Heminges, Burbage, Condell and the others.

For that reason our anti-Stratfordian friends strive mightily to discredit them—and once more ask us to "forget for awhile the thing called evidence" and accept in its stead their own unsupported theory, this time a theory that strains credulity far beyond the breaking point.

The bequests to the actors were interlineated, between the lines of the original draft of the will. Our anti-Stratfordian friends, desiring to discredit them, ask us to believe that they were criminally inserted in the will by someone other than Shakespeare, so as to help that great "hoax" which was to come out seven years later in 1623, the *First Folio.* The great conspirators, they ask us to believe, were already in 1616 when Shakespeare died, planning to bring out the *First Folio* as "William Shakespeare's" so as to deceive the public as to the real authorship, and were planning to have his old fellow actors state in it, as they did, that Shakespeare of Stratford was the author. To make that statement seem all the more truthful it would help to have those bequests to the actors in the will.

The *American Bar Association Journal,* November, 1959, p. 1228, refers to these bequests and says:

> "They are in an interlineation, added some time later, no one knows when, not even whether it was before or after the death of the testator."

The Ogburns in their *Shakespeare, The Real Man Behind The Name,* go into detail. It is their theory, as it was also Looney's in *"Shakespeare" Identified,* that the great conspirators had Ben Jonson go up to Stratford and arrange for that criminal interlineation to be made. How they knew Shakespeare was about to die they do not tell us. However, it is generally believed that Ben Jonson did go to Stratford and call on Shakespeare shortly before he died, because the Reverend John Ward in 1662 became Rector of Shakespeare's church in Stratford and in his note-books, still extant, says that "Shakespeare, Drayton, and Ben Jonson had a merry meeting and it seems drank too hard, for Shakespeare died of a fever there contracted." Weaving that into their theory, the Ogburns tell us, page 130:

> "He" (i.e., Jonson) "arranges with Digges, whose step-father, it seems, has supervision of Shaksper's will, to have a line inserted in the will making Heminge, Condell and Burbage a bequest..."

That is the theory, wholly without evidentiary support, which they would have us accept in lieu of the documented evidence of the will itself.

In asking us to accept that theory, which makes both Ben Jonson and young Leonard Digges criminals, our anti-Stratfordian friends seem to have overlooked how pointless for their purposes such an interlineation would have been. Why did Jonson bother to do it? It could not have served the great conspirators' purpose, because not one potential reader of the *First Folio* could ever possibly have seen the will. It was probated in 1616, and remained hidden in the files of the probate court for well over a century till discovered in 1747. *(Chambers,* Vol. II, p. 169.) Just how could it have served Jonson's alleged purpose to deceive? How was anyone to know about it? The anti-Stratfordian argument based on it is clearly pointless.

In addition, a close look at a photograph of Shakespeare's will, reproduced in *Chambers* and many other books, seems clearly to show that there were a number of interlineations and all in the same handwriting. Were they all added "some time later"? Or did Ben Jonson "some time later" seek out the scrivener who had made the other interlineations and get him to interline the ones for the actors too? A rather dangerous game for Ben to have played—too many people in on it, and someone might land in jail.

Furthermore, many great handwriting experts have studied the will, but not one has ever suggested that it was thus tampered with; yet that is the theory our anti-Stratfordian friends would have us accept.

The will is powerful documentary proof that Shakespeare regarded Heminges, Burbage and Condell, the then three survivors of the old Chamberlain's Company Group, as his "Fellowe" Actors.

VII

His Stratford Monument

HIS Stratford monument, in Stratford's Holy Trinity Church, was erected at some point between his death in 1616 and the issuance of the *First Folio* in 1623, for it is referred to in the *First Folio*.

On the monument the following words are carved in stone:

> "Stay Passenger, why goest thou by so fast?
> Read if thou canst, whom envious Death hath plast,
> With in this monument Shakspeare: with whome
> Quick Nature dide; whose name doth deck this Tombe,
> Far more then cost; sith all that He hath writt,
> Leaves living art, but page, to serve his witt.
> Obit. Ano. Do. 1616
> Aetatis 53 Die 23 Apr."

It will be noted that the monument spells his name "Shakspeare," the sometimes Stratford spelling, not "Shakespeare," the more usual London spelling. This would seem to indicate that it was erected by his contemporaries in Stratford, not by any conspirators in London. And there, in words carved in stone, his contemporaries tell us that he it was who was the writer.

Convinced as they are that his authorship was "impossible,"

yet faced with this massive documentary evidence to the contrary, our anti-Stratfordian friends, struggle very hard to explain the monument away. They offer three theories for that purpose.

One is that it was all part of the great "plot" (see Chapter XII, *infra*)—that the great conspirators in London, psychopathically anxious even at that late date to hide the true authorship, erected the monument so as to deceive the public.

Thus it is that the *American Bar Association Journal*, May, 1960, p. 522, pictures the great conspirators "erecting a monument in Stratford church, with a craftily worded inscription upon it to mystify the populace."

In asking us to "forget for awhile" the evidence of those words carved by his contemporaries in stone, and in its stead accept the theory that the great conspirators were so anxious to hide the true authorship that they actually had that monument fraudulently erected (and with not one shred of evidence to sustain the theory), our anti-Stratfordian friends again seem to have reached one of their finest hours.

Their second theory is that Shakespeare himself was so clever at deception that he fooled his Stratford contemporaries into believing he was the author—hence the statue. Again there is no evidence whatsoever to support such a surmise.

Their third theory is that the bust seen there today is not the original bust. The words carved in stone are the revealing evidence, and even our anti-Stratfordian friends do not theorize that they are not the original words—but even in claiming that the bust itself is new they are demonstrably wrong.

The bust shows Shakespeare, pen in hand, writing, with a tasseled pillow under his manuscript. In 1656 Sir W. Dugdale put out a book called Dugdale's *Antiquities of Warwickshire* (appearing again in 1730), and in it gives many pictures, drawn by him, of monuments in Warwickshire. One is a picture of the Shakespeare monument, and it differs greatly in appearance from the bust seen there today. ~~Our anti-Stratfordian friends~~ claim that this shows that the present bust replaced the one drawn by Dugdale. Even Dugdale's drawing showed that the words carved in stone are still the original words, which is the important point. But the bust is still the original, never changed.

It is known documentarily that in 1748-49 the statue was cleaned and "repaired," and it is the contention of our anti-Stratfordian friends that in the "repair" job an entirely new bust replaced the original one.

On this point the *American Bar Association Journal* made what was probably its worst lapse-from sound scholarship. For in its issue of February, 1959, on page 145, it categorically informed the lawyers of America that in 1747 (incidentally, the wrong year) the original bust "was replaced with the bust seen in the church today," and categorically repeated that bit of misinformation on page 146.

In *Shakespeare, The Real Man Behind The Name,* the Ogburns initially fell into that same error, for on page 68 they said of the bust:

> "It was removed in 1747 and replaced by the present representation..."

But the Ogburns learned of their error in time to retract the statement, for in a loose sheet of "errata" accompanying their book they withdrew it and say:

> "The categorical statement that the bust was replaced in 1747 is unwarranted. It is a matter of interpretation ..."

They do not say what it is "a matter of interpretation" of.

It has been pointed out many times over the years that Dugdale in his drawings was a wholly unreliable reporter of fact. In that same *Antiquities* are drawings by him of other contemporary statues which are still extant and many of them are extremely inaccurate, some even more inaccurate than the one of the Shakespeare bust. In the *Antiquities* Dugdale was reporting for a very large area. He made sketches, possibly sometimes even from memory, and from them the engravings were made, with many enormous errors creeping in.

In any event, the contemporary documents clarify the matter. As Sir Edmond Chambers puts it (*Chambers,* Vol. II, p. 185), the theory of replacement "gets no support from the Stratford documents."

The conclusive document is the one written in September, 1749, when the "repair" job had just been done, by Joseph Greene, headmaster of the Stratford Grammar School that year, printed in full in Gibson's *The Shakespeare Claimants,* p. 257, saying:

> "In repairing the whole (which was done by contribution of ye Neighborhood early in ye current year) Care was taken, as nearly as cou'd be, not to add or to diminish what ye work consisted of, & appear'd to be when first erected; and really, except for changing ye Substance of ye Architraves from white Alabaster to white Marble, nothing has been done but supplying with ye original materials whatsoever was by Accident broken off; reviving the old Colouring, and renewing the Gilding that was lost."

As to the words carved in stone, which constitute the real evidence, Dugdale in his drawing did not give them but represented them with dotted lines. These, says Mr. Gibson in *The Shakespeare Claimants,* page 254, "correspond exactly with the existing arrangement, except that the date has been omitted."

If our anti-Stratfordian friends want further documented proof that no change in the monument was made in 1748, they should look at the engraving of the monument made from a sketch by Virtue and published in 1725, before the "repairs" of 1748, showing that the monument looked much then as it looks today. The engraving is reproduced on page 32 of *The Man of Stratford—The Real Shakespeare,* By Mr. W. K. Montague.

VIII

The First Folio

FOLLOWING hard upon the over-
whelming proof given by his Stratford monument came further
overwhelming proof in 1623, with the publication of the *First
Folio.*

Shakespeare of Stratford died in 1616; Richard Burbage in
1619. That left but two survivors of his old fellow actors, namely
John Heminges and Henry Condell. They were to live for a
number of years longer, and were highly respected men.

Those two it was who brought out the *First Folio*, with him
stated to have been the author, publishing in the single volume
all of his plays. In their introduction they make it crystal clear
that publication of the plays was a labor of love for their de-
parted fellow actor, William Shakespeare, who wrote them.

In the preliminary leaves of the *First Folio* memorial poems
to Shakespeare by several eminent writers of the day were
printed, including poems by Leonard Digges and Ben Jonson.
They, as well as Heminges and Condell, state without equivocation that the author of the plays was William Shakespeare of
Stratford-on-Avon, the actor.

A.

The Testimony of Heminges and Condell

Of all people then alive, Heminges and Condell were in the best, the perfect, position to know whether Shakespeare of Stratford was or was not the author. For over twenty years they had worked intimately with him in the theatre, producing and acting in these very plays. Had he been a fraud, palming off onto his Company as his own plays written by someone else he could not have fooled them—could not have fooled them through one rehearsal, to say nothing of thirty-six plays over twenty years. Without equivocation they advise us that they were "his playes," their exact words being that they were bringing out the *First Folio* (*Chambers*, Vol. II, p. 228):

> ". . . without ambition either of selfe-profit, or fame; onely to keepe the memory of so worthy a Friend & Fellow alive, as was our Shakespeare, by humble offer of his playes . . ."

With those words they make it clear that the author was their friend and fellow actor, and that their publication of "his playes" was a labor of love.

They tell us more. In a letter printed in the *First Folio* addressed to the "great Variety of Readers," they further reveal their own emotional involvement with these words:

> "It had been a thing, we confesse, worthie to have bene wished, that the Author himselfe had liv'd to have set forth, and overseen his owne writings; But since it hath been ordained otherwise, and he by death departed from that right, we pray you do not envie his Friends, the office of their care, and paine, to have collected & published them. . . . Who, as he was a happie imitator of Nature, was a most gentle expresser of it. His mind and hand went together; And what he thought, he uttered with that easiness, that wee have scarce received from him a blot on his papers."

They also said still more, and in doing so dealt a death-blow, obviously without realizing it, to the claims of every one of our pretenders. For they dedicated the *First Folio* to the Earl of Pembroke and the Earl of Montgomery because, they said, the two Earls had loved the plays and "have prosecuted both them, and their author living, with so much favour."

Thus they documentarily inform us that during his lifetime the author of these plays had been shown "much favour" by those two youthful Earls. It could not have been Oxford whom they had "prosecuted" with so much favor, because Oxford outranked both of them in the nobility and, in addition, Oxford was older than they by some thirty years, and was the father-in-law of Montgomery. Nor could they have been referring to Bacon, for he was still alive. And Marlowe had permanently disappeared in 1593, when these two Earls were still children. It was, it had to have been, the "upstart Crow" from Stratford whom they had so honored while living.

Clearer testimony, by more reliable witnesses in perfect position to know, could not be imagined. They were "his playes," Shakespeare's, their "Friend & Fellow" actor.

Our anti-Stratfordian friends cannot answer the testimony of Heminges and Condell. Accordingly, convinced that Shakespeare's authorship was "impossible" and that hence there *must* be *some* answer, they fall back, as they are compelled to do, on their "plot" theory. (See Chapter XII, *infra.*) Heminges and Condell, they tell us, were in on the "plot" and were lying for pay.

To support this theory, they point out that in their introduction to the *First Folio* Heminges and Condell state that Shakespeare wrote so rapidly and smoothly that his manuscripts were handed to the actors with scarcely a blot on them—and certainly Heminges and Condell clearly implied that the *First Folio* was printed from those manuscripts. They, our anti-Stratfordian friends, ignore the fact that by 1621, when printing of the *First Folio* was begun, every one of those original manuscripts was from nine to thirty years old and had, over the years, received much handling from the many actors who had so often used them. Hence any manuscript, even if perfect when received, had long since ceased to be so.

In any event, the *First Folio* was demonstrably printed from playhouse copies, with interlineations, alterations and additions that have puzzled scholars for centuries, with ten of the plays copied into the *First Folio* directly from previously printed Quarto editions.

From this it is clear that Heminges and Condell, in giving the impression that the printing was straight from unblemished original manuscripts may well be accused of having been something less than forthright. They made what might be called exaggerated "sales talk"—and that, say our anti-Stratfordian friends, finishes them off.

The real villain in the affair, our anti-Stratfordian friends would have us believe, was Ben Jonson. He it was, they say, who was hired by the great conspirators to bring out this "hoax," the *First Folio*, and he hired Heminges and Condell to lend their names to the fraud, to give verisimilitude and deceive all readers. The document, as we shall shortly see, in which Ben Jonson long after the *First Folio*, speaks for himself, totally destroys that theory.

The very printing errors in the *First Folio*, the very carelessness that is apparent throughout its pages, all of which is pointed to by our anti-Stratfordian friends as showing that Heminges and Condell were lying, is in actual fact clear proof that no great conspirators in London were behind its publication. Had they been, they would surely have seen to it that a more deceptively careful job was done.

B.

The Testimony of Leonard Digges

Among the memorial poems printed in the *First Folio* was one by Leonard Digges, stating that the plays were written by Shakespeare of Stratford. In Leonard Digges we have an unimpeachable witness of towering stature.

The complete identity and background of Leonard Digges was not known until 1937, when Dr. Leslie Hotson published it in his *I, William Shakespeare*, with impeccable documentation. He was a young aristocrat who grew up from the age of twelve in the manor Alderminster, on Stratford's outskirts, where he came in 1600 to live in the home of his step-father, Thomas Russell. And the step-father was on such intimate terms with Shakespeare of Stratford that the latter appointed him testamentary overseer in his will. Accordingly it is impossible that the young Leonard Digges did not at least know who Shakespeare of Stratford was and what his reputation was.

By 1621, when printing of the *First Folio* was begun, he was thirty-three years old, with an already established reputation as a poet in his own right, in permanent residence as a translator at University College, Oxford, and with some years in the British Diplomatic Corps behind him. A more honorable, highly educated witness, in possession of all the facts, would have been impossible to find. Naturally enough, because of his background and established poetic ability, Heminges and Condell, as they were getting memorial poems for the *First Folio*, turned for one to him.

He wrote two memorial poems to Shakespeare, one of which was published in the *First Folio*, the other some years later. The one in the *First Folio* reads as follows:

b

"To the Memorie
of the deceased Authour Maister
W. Shakespeare

"*Shake-speare*, at length thy pious fellowes give
The world thy Workes; thy Workes, by which, out-live
Thy Tombe, thy name must; when that stone is rent,
And Time dissolves thy *Stratford* moniment,
Here we alive shall view thee still. This Booke,
When Brasse and Marble fade, shall make thee looke
Fresh to all Ages; when Posteritie
Shall loath what's new, thinke all is prodegie
That is not *Shake-speares*; ev'ry Line, each Verse,
Here shall revive, redeeme thee from thy Herse.
Nor Fire, nor cankring Age, as *Naso* said,
Of his, thy wit-fraught Booke shall once invade,
Nor shall I e're beleeve, or thinke thee dead
(Though mist) untill our bankrout Stage be sped
(Impossible) with some new strain t'out-do
Passions of *Juliet*, and her *Romeo*;
Or till I heare a Scene more nobly take,
Then when thy half-Sword parlying *Romans* spake,
Till these, till any of thy Volumes rest
Shall with more fire, more feeling be exprest,
Be sure, our *Shake-speare*, thou canst never dye,
But crown'd with Lawrell, live eternally."

Thus we see this Stratford-raised young aristocrat, aware of Shakespeare's Stratford monument which he mentions, stating unequivocally that it was Shakespeare of Stratford who was the author.

The poem seems clearly to have been written from an overflowing heart by a young poet who knew and revered him. For Shakespeare, "our Shake-speare," he says, was personally missed and for him could never die.

It is of interest to note that he tells us in this poem that Shakespeare the author was also an actor for, as he puts it, "at length thy pious fellowes" give the world the plays. And in this single poem he spells the name "Shakespeare" once and "Shake-speare" three times, clearly showing that no distinction is to be made between the hyphenated and unhyphenated forms.

Again our anti-Stratfordian friends are unable to answer this unimpeachable testimony, hence again they are compelled to fall back on their "plot" theory. (See Chapter XII, *infra.*) Leonard Digges was in on the "plot" and was lying for pay, they would have us believe.

The *American Bar Association Journal,* September, 1959, pages 995-6, tells us that Leonard Digges' poem, above quoted, was "a paid advertisement to take in the general public;" and the Ogburns, in their *Shakespeare, The Real Man Behind The Name,* page 130, tell us that Leonard Digges no doubt collaborated with Ben Jonson and, via his step-father who was overseer of Shakespeare's will, got the bequests to the three actors "inserted" in the will.

Thus they would have us accept, instead of the documented evidence, their theory that Leonard Digges not only lied for money by writing a false "paid advertisement", but also joined Ben Jonson in a crime by inserting a false (and, for their purposes, totally useless) entry in the Stratford man's will. That is sheer character assassination, unsupported by the slightest scintilla of evidence.

It is of interest, and somewhat further revealing, that in 1622, when printing of the *First Folio* had begun but was not yet completed, Leonard Digges published a book of his own, his translation of the Spanish book *Gerardo, the Unfortunate Spaniard,* and in dedicating it to the two Herbert brothers, the Earl of Pembroke and the Earl of Montgomery, referred to them as " 'the incomparable pair of brethren' of Heminges' and Condell's forthcoming Folio of Shakespeare." (*I, William Shakespeare,* p. 243.)

Thus Leonard Digges refers to the *First Folio* as the "forth-coming" project of "Heminges' and Condell's," and he spoke from personal knowledge, for he knew both Heminges and Condell, was at Oxford with Heminges' son, and in addition knew the Earls of Pembroke and Montgomery (all thoroughly documented in *I, William Shakespeare*).

One further poem by Leonard Digges praising Shakespeare as the author was published in 1640, five years after Digges' death. It is printed in full by Sir Edmund Chambers (*Chambers*, Vol. II, p. 232). In it his personal love of the man Shakespeare of Stratford is again revealed, for the poem begins with the following words:

> "Poets are borne not made, when I would prove
> This truth, the glad remembrance I must love
> Of never dying *Shakespeare*, who alone,
> Is argument enough to make that one."

So, he loved the *"glad remembrance"* of Shakespeare of Stratford.

And in this second poem he seems to be telling us that he personally saw Shakespeare in the very act of composition. For, says he in the poem, it was not "work" for Shakespeare "to contrive a play." The exact words of the poem are (speaking of his published plays):

> "First, that he was a Poet none would doubt,
> That heard th' applause of what he sees set out
> Imprinted; where thou hast (I will not say)
> Reader his Workes (for to contrive a Play
> To him twas none) the patterne of all wit,
> Art without Art unparaleled as yet."

Thus at one point Ben Jonson has told us that Shakespeare, the actor and poet, "flowed with facility"; his fellow actors Heminges and Condell that he wrote with "easiness"; and

Leonard Digges that it was not work for him "to contrive a play." Were they or were they not eye-witnesses? The actors and Ben Jonson clearly were; quite probably Leonard Digges was too.

To induce us to "forget for awhile" the documented evidence that gives us Leonard Digges' testimony and accept in its stead the theory that this honorable and high class young aristocrat, raised in Stratford, was lying for money and had criminally collaborated in altering a will, surely requires evidence to support it—but none has ever been forthcoming.

C.

The Testimony of Ben Jonson

In Ben Jonson, too, playwright of Shakespeare's day, we have another witness of towering stature, second only in importance to Heminges, Condell and Leonard Digges.

In 1616, the year of Shakespeare's death, Jonson published his *Workes*, and in that book stated that in 1598 his *Every Man In His Humour* was produced by the Chamberlain's Company with "Will. Shakespeare" one of the "principall Comoedians," adding that at Christmas, 1603, his *Sejanus* was produced by the King's Men, with "Will. Shake-Speare" one of the "principall Tragoedians." (*Chambers*, Vol. II, pp. 71-72.)

Thus we see that since as early as 1598 Ben Jonson had worked with Shakespeare in the theatre. We also see, incidentally, that Jonson spelled his name once "Will. Shakespeare", and once in hyphenated form "Will. Shake-Speare", showing how the two forms were sometimes interchangeably used.

On the title page of the *First Folio* appeared the Droeshout etching showing the now universally known picture of Shakespeare, and on the opposite page was Ben Jonson's well-known short poem regarding it, stating that "The Figure that thou here seest put, It was for gentle Shakespeare cut."

In addition to that short introductory poem Jonson also wrote a far longer one, printed in the *First Folio,* in lavish praise of Shakespeare.

It began:

> "To the memory of my beloved,
> The Author
> Mr. William Shakespeare
> and
> What he hath left us.

> "To draw no envy (*Shakespeare*) on thy name,
> Am I thus ample to thy Booke, and Fame:
> While I confesse thy writings to be such,
> As neither *Man,* nor *Muse,* can praise too much."

He continued this poem for seventy-six more lines, many now universally familiar, in which he called Shakespeare "Soule of the Age," hailed him as the "Sweet Swan of Avon," and stated that "He was not of an age, but for all time." He commented also on his "small Latine, and lesse Greeke." (*Chambers,* Vol. II, pp. 207 et seq.)

Our anti-Stratfordian friends cannot answer Ben Jonson's testimony, but they strive mightily to do so. In fact, it is Jonson, they theorize, who must have been the villian in the whole affair—the one who master-minded the *First Folio* "hoax" for pay from the Earl of Pembroke.

As to how, when and how much Jonson was paid for this the *American Bar Association Journal,* November, 1959, p. 1229, tells us:

> "In 1621, when Jonson was financially hard pressed, and the First Folio was being prepared for publication, the Earl of Pembroke increased Jonson's stipend temporarily to 200 pounds, or about $8,000 in our money."

In its issue of May, 1960, page 522, the *Journal* widened the payees of this sum to include Heminges and Condell, telling us that there was paid to "Ben Jonson, Heminge and Condell a total of some two hundred pounds."

It was, they theorize, that sum of 200 pounds which was paid to induce Jonson to play his long and complicated role of trickery and deception that culminated in the great "hoax," the *First Folio*. For that sum he fraudulently entered in his *Workes*, published in 1616, the two instances above-quoted where Shakespeare acted in two of Jonson's plays; he criminally got the bequests to the three fellow actors interlined into Shakespeare's will, inducing Leonard Digges to help him get that done; he got Heminges and Condell to let him use their names so as to give his fraudulent statements in the *First Folio* verisimilitude; and he wrote all of his poetry in the *First Folio* with tongue-in-cheek, using *double-entendre* which our anti-Stratfordian friends insist is clearly there for those in the know to see. As to the alleged fraudulent erection of the Stratford monument, Jonson's connection with that does not appear.

However, out of that same 200 pounds he must have had to pay off Heminges and Condell, not to mention Leonard Digges for his "paid advertisement." Money went a long way in those days.

To support this complicated theory our anti-Stratfordian friends are somewhat hard-pressed for evidence. It has been many times pointed out that the rather flowery dedication of the *First Folio* to the two Earls, signed by Heminges and Condell, seems in part a paraphrase of the dedication of Pliny's *Natural History*. Since that required translation from Latin, and since Ben Jonson was not only a professional writer but also an able Latin scholar, this gives meager ground for believing that Ben Jonson helped Heminges and Condell in writing their dedication. That, our anti-Stratfordian friends theorize, shows how fraudulent the entire thing was—all a "hoax" cooked up by Ben Jonson. That is the extent of their "evidence."

To give further support to their "hoax" theory, our anti-Stratfordian friends also point out what they call the obvious *double-entendre* of all the poetry Ben Jonson wrote for the *First Folio*. One or two examples of that may be enlightening.

Thus, in the *First Folio* Ben Jonson's introductory poem reads as follows:

"To the Reader.

"The Figure, that thou here seest put,
    It was for gentle Shakespeare cut;
    Wherein the Graver had a strife
    With Nature, to out-doo the life;
    O, could he have but drawne his wit
    As well in brasse, as he hath hit
    His face, the Print would then surpasse
    All that was ever writ in brasse.
    But, since he cannot, Reader, looke
    Not on his Picture, but his Booke."

That little poem does seem to be a clear statement that the etching looked like Shakespeare (and certainly it did not look like any of the pretenders) and that the plays in the book were written by the same Shakespeare. But, says the *American Bar Association Journal*, to read it that way is to miss its *double-entendre* and to fail to see the "wink" with which Ben Jonson is tipping off those in the know. That poem, says the *Journal*, September, 1959, page 995, should be interpreted to read as follows (italics the *Journal's*):

His Face, the Print would then surpass
"This *Outline* that thou here seest put,
    It was for *high-born* Shakespeare cut,
    Wherein the Graver had a strife
    With *Reality, travestying* the Life;
    O, could he but have drawn his Wit
    As *brashly* and *boldly* as he has *hid*
All that was *E. Ver* shown (here) in a Brazen Hoax."

67

The *Journal* author's muse does seem to have deserted him a bit at the poem's end, but the meaning is clear—"white" must be read to mean "black." The "E. Ver" in the last full line, from the word "ever" used by Ben Jonson, is Edward de Vere, Seventeenth Earl of Oxford.

In explaining this re-write of the poem the *Journal* then goes on to tell us:

> "To begin with, the Droeshout engraving could hardly be a representation of the supreme poet of the English race. That it was not meant to be taken seriously is apparent from the fact that the face is covered by a mask which shows along the edge of the jaw and has a tab for the ear. The clothes are absurd: one sleeve is put in backwards, and there is no neck beneath the preposterous collar. Jonson's verse, *To the Reader*, is equally ambiguous. The discerning reader was expected to penetrate the double intent."

This seems to be telling us that the great conspirators wanted both to eat their cake and have it too. They wanted to fool the people as to the authorship, but didn't want to fool everybody— wanted the insiders to see the joke.

In that same article the *American Bar Association Journal* tells us also of the "double intent" to be seen in Ben Jonson's longer poem in the *First Folio*. In that longer poem, the *Journal* tells us, Jonson wrote the first few lines with Shakespeare of Stratford in mind, then, without telling us just when he was changing, he wrote the last lines, where all the praise is found, about the "real" Shakespeare, the great unknown. That does seem odd, but, says the *Journal* (September, 1959, p. 996):

> ". . . Ben Jonson makes a *volte-face*, and, in a spirit of devotion to truth, gives us the real Shakespeare, the supreme poet, in his Introductory Poem."

In other words, once more our anti-Stratfordian friends are

compelled to fall back on their "plot" theory (see Chapter XII, *infra*). "Let's forget for a while this documented evidence from eye-witnesses and accept in its stead our unsupported theories that Heminges, Condell, Ben Jonson and Leonard Digges all were lying for pay."

Fortunately, some years after the *First Folio*, Ben Jonson speaks for himself, and so completely does he demolish the "plot" theory, and so important are his words, that they should be read in full by everyone who seeks the incontrovertible story of the authorship.

In *Timber*, published from his note-books in 1641, some eighteen years after the *First Folio*, he wrote the following, obviously for "posterity" (printed in *Chambers*, Vol. II, page 210):

> "I *remember*, the Players have often mentioned it as an honour to *Shakespeare*, that in his writing, (whatsoever he penn'd) hee never blotted out line. My answer hath beene, would he had blotted out a thousand. Which they thought a malevolent speech. I had not told posterity this, but for their ignorance, who choose that circumstance to commend their friend by, wherein he most faulted. And to justifie mine owne candor, (for I lov'd the man, and doe honour his memory on this side Idolatry) as much as any. Hee was (indeed) honest, and of an open, and free nature; had an excellent *Phantsie;* brave notions, and gentle expressions; wherein he flow'd with that facility, that sometime it was necessary he should be stop'd: *Sufflaminandus erat,* as *Augustus* said of *Haterius.* His wit was in his owne power; would the rule of it had beene so too. Many times hee fell into those things, could not escape laughter. As when hee said in the person of *Caesar,* one speaking to him: *Caesar thou dost me wrong.* Hee replyed: *Caesar did never wrong, but with just cause* and such like; which were ridiculous. But hee redeemed his vices, with his virtues. There was ever more in him to be praysed then to be pardoned."

Here, writing to tell "posterity," Jonson could not have been trying to further any "plot." Had that been his purpose, and the purpose of the *First Folio*, he had only to keep quiet. But instead he chose to speak and to leave this priceless document to posterity.

IX

The Cost of Publishing the First Folio

THE cost alone of publishing the *First Folio* proves its fraudulence—so runs one anti-Stratfordian theory. It was astronomical, they say, proving that some hidden member of the nobility was paying it.

The *American Bar Association Journal* tells us this more than once. In the issue of November, 1959, page 1229, it says that the deficit from the printing was "far beyond the resources of the avowed editors, Heminge and Condell", and adds:

> "Quite obviously, the financing of the Folio must have come from the outside."

Then in its issue of May, 1960, at page 522, the *Journal* goes into more detail, with the following:

> "It can be shown conclusively that it was the Herbert brothers" (i.e., the Earls of Pembroke and Montgomery) "who in 1623 bore the staggering loss that attended the publication of the 'Shakespeare' First Folio. No one else involved had money to lose. The cost of the work has been set at close to 6,000

pounds, a great fortune in those days. It was printed on gilt-edged paper and bound in embossed leather. The clergy raved—no Bible had ever been so luxuriously bound! Six hundred copies were sold at twenty-two shillings each. The printers, who had been bankrupt in 1620, worked two years on the type setting, solvent, even affluent."

This material is woven by our anti-Stratfordian friends into their "plot" theory. The Earls of Pembroke and Montgomery, the theory is, wanted the plays printed so that the public could have them, but did not want the true authorship known. Hence they had the job done ostensibly by Heminges and Condell, but the two Earls bore "the staggering financial loss."

If the cost of printing the *First Folio* came up to 6,000 pounds, as stated above by the *Journal*, that meant a cost of approximately a quarter of a million dollars, as measured today. If the two Earls put up any such sum, and watched it go down the drain, they were surely anxious to get the plays published—and to keep the authorship dark.

But if it caused so huge a financial loss, why was it that the same printing firm brought out a second edition in just nine years? Did those same two Earls put up another quarter of a million dollars for the second edition? If so, why? The first edition had already given the plays to the public. The second edition could only have been for profit. Yet out it came in nine years—followed shortly by a third edition.

Willoughby puts it this way in his *A Printer of Shakespeare*, p. 165:

"... the volume sold so well that in 1632 Jaggard's successor, Richard Cotes, issued a second edition."

Vast research has been done on the *First Folio*, is, in fact, still being done, and much is known about it. But there are two things which even today no one knows—how many copies were printed and how much it cost.

The most recent and most erudite book on the subject is *The Printing and Proof-Reading of the First Folio of Shakespeare,* by Charlton Hinman, two volumes, printed in 1963. There it is pointed out that in 1821 it was believed that only 250 copies had been printed—but almost that number are known to be extant today. By 1909 it was believed that about 500 copies had been printed. Today the estimated number is between 1,000 and 1,500 copies. In his book (Vol. I, p. 39) Mr. Hinman says:

> "As Greg pointed out many years ago, the production of the book cannot have been commercially profitable unless about this number of copies" (i.e., 1,000) "could be sold; and it can hardly be doubted that for Jaggard and his associates, if not for Heminge and Condell and other Shakespeare's fellows of the theatre, the Folio was essentially a business venture—and, indeed, a successful one. It must at any rate have sold well, since a second edition was issued in 1632, only nine years after the first."

Thus we see that the anti-Stratfordian theory that the cost of the *First Folio* proves it was secretly financed by the Earls of Pembroke and Montgomery has no foundation of fact. No one knows just what the cost of the publication was—but that it made, rather than lost, money seems clearly evident from the same printing firm's having brought out a second edition in just nine years.

X

The Stratford Documents

NOTHING that happened in Stratford prior to his death has any direct bearing on the question of authorship. The documents there refer exclusively to minor matters, to lawsuits for the collection of small sums, and to his purchases of real estate.

It has been claimed by Looney, in his *"Shakespeare" Identified*, that by 1597 he had permanently retired to Stratford from London, but that is patently erroneous. He did return to Stratford in 1597 and bought New Place, the most imposing house in town. However, he didn't stay; he returned to London. In 1598 he joined with his fellow actors in London in hi-jacking the *Theatre*; from 1602 to 1604, as shown by his own affidavit in the *Belott-Mountjoy* litigation (see Chapter XIII, B, *infra*), he was living in London, on Silver Street; and Cuthbert Burbage has told us that even as late as 1608 he was still one of the "men Players."

Our anti-Stratfordian friends put forward the theory that since the Stratford documents show that on one occasion he speculated in malt, on one occasion sold a small amount of malt and sued for the purchase price, several times brought suit to collect small sums, and several times invested substantial sums in Stratford real property, he was too interested in money to have been the great poet.

That, of course, is nonsense. All that those Stratford documents show is that having known poverty once he had no intention of knowing it again.

That there were aristocratic families in Stratford, and that as he grew in fame they welcomed him and sought his company is clear from the Stratford documents.

The aristocratic Stratford family with which he was most demonstrably friendly was the Combe family. Their pedigree and history are given by Sir Edmund Chambers, who deemed them important enough to devote fourteen pages to them. (*Chambers*, Vol. II, pp. 127 et seq.)

In 1602 he bought from William and John Combe "the old Stratford Freehold" for three hundred and twenty pounds. In 1605 he bought for four hundred and forty pounds a substantial leasehold interest in "the Stratford tithes," in which the Combe family owned an equal interest. In 1613 John Combe in his will left "to Mr. William Shackspeare five pounds." And in 1616 in his own will Shakespeare bequeathed "to Mr. Thomas Combe my sword." His relationship with them was obviously friendly.

The other aristocratic family in Stratford with whom he was also demonstrably friendly was that of Thomas Russell, the second son of Sir Thomas Russell. The history of this younger Thomas Russell is thoroughly documented for us by Dr. Leslie Hotson in his *I, William Shakespeare.*

Shakespeare, as we have seen, was on such intimate terms in that wealthy and aristocratic household that he appointed Thomas Russell testamentary overseer in his will. And, most important of all, as we have also seen, Leonard Digges was this Thomas Russell's step-son, and grew up in Russell's Stratford estate "Alderminster" from 1600, having come there in that year at the age of twelve.

Shakespeare's reputation in Stratford is also clearly revealed for us in the notebooks of the Reverend John Ward, who came to Stratford in 1662 as Rector of Holy Trinity Church, where Shakespeare's monument is. His notebooks are now in the Folger Library in Washington, and among many memoranda in them concerning medicine, theology and people he had met or heard about, are four entries about Shakespeare and his family. Largely they are gossip the Reverend Ward had picked up, such as:

> "Shakespeare, Drayton, and Ben Jonson had a merry meeting and it seems drank too hard, for Shakespeare died of a fever there contracted."

Shakespeare had by Reverend Ward's day been dead some fifty years, but his grand-daughter Lady Bernard was still alive and Reverend Ward mentions her name but does not state that he got his information from her or that he had even met her. She was then living in Abingdon. But it is from that entry in Reverend Ward's notebook that we see that, at least in Stratford's gossip, Ben Jonson and Drayton came to Stratford and called on Shakespeare. They would hardly have come to call on some nonentity.

But it is Reverend Ward's further entry that is so revealing of the talk still going on in Stratford—and surely if anyone in Stratford heard all the local talk it was the local Rector of the local Episcopal Church. In his notebook Reverend Ward wrote to himself the following reminder:

> "Remember to peruse Shakespeare's plays and be versed in them that I may not be ignorant in that matter."

Here we have wholly unimpeachable testimony that among

76

the people of Stratford there was no question as to who wrote them. Certainly the Reverend Ward was not writing this in his notebook to help further the "plot" theory; and certainly it was to Shakespeare of Stratford he was referring, since he tells us that Lady Bernard was his grand-daughter. This is testimony that by no possible theory can be rationalized away by our anti-Stratfordian friends.

And since the Rector felt he must "be versed" in Shakespeare's plays "that I may not be ignorant in that matter" it was clearly so that he could hold his own in the local conversations about them, still obviously locally going on.

The Shakespeare coat-of-arms may also be deemed a Stratford document, for the arms shown on his Stratford monument agree in every detail with the arms granted to his father.

In fact, it is in a priceless document, related to the coat-of-arms grant, that we have what so many of our anti-Stratfordian friends seem unaware of—namely, a wholly unimpeachable tie-in between Shakespeare of Stratford and Shakespeare the Player. This is of considerable importance, as we seek the incontrovertible story, for it is sometimes carelessly stated that there is no proof (despite the overwhelming proof) that the man from Stratford and the London actor were the same man.

In 1602 a quarrel arose in the College of Heralds, in which some of the Heralds were attacked by others for having been too free and easy in the granting of coats-of-arms; and the grant to Shakespeare's father was cited as one example. (See Chute, *Shakespeare of London*, p. 185; also *Chambers*, Vol. II, p. 24.) One of the attacking Heralds was Ralph Brooke, York Herald, and in the very course of the quarrel a document, still extant, was written giving a sketch of the Shakespeare coat-of-arms, and below it, thought to be in the handwriting of Ralph Brooke himself, the words "Shakespear ye Player." A photograph of that priceless document is set forth on page 47 of the Folger Library's booklet entitled "The Authorship of Shakespeare," obtainable by mail for one dollar. And a photograph of it is the frontispiece of this book.

Here we see, in a document whose authenticity cannot be questioned, and which cannot be rationalized away even with the "plot" theory, the incontrovertible proof that Shakespeare of Stratford and Shakespeare the Player were one and the same man.

XI

Inaccuracies With Which Anti-Stratfordian Writers Clutter, or at Least Obfuscate, the Record

A.

That His Name Was Not "Shakespeare"

This is a basic tenet to which most, if not all, anti-Stratfordian writers cling—that his name was "Shaksper," not "Shakespeare." Hence he was not the "Shakespeare" who was the author.

Thus the *American Bar Association Journal*, February, 1959, page 143, refers to him as "Shaksper" and categorically states that that "was the name he himself used." Actually, not one known instance exists where he used that name—where he either spelled his own name that way or signed any document in which his name was spelled that way. The statement is simply not true.

Again in its issue of March, 1959, page 240, the *Journal* repeats its error and says: "The Stratford man was named Shaksper, never Shakespeare."

The documented record teems with proof to the contrary.

In 1613 he purchased the Gate-House in London, with two original copies of the deed-of-purchase, one of which is in the Folger Library in Washington whence for $5 a photographic copy of it is obtainable by mail. In that deed he *had* to tell the professional scrivener who prepared it what his name was. It is spelled "William Shakespeare," and he signed it.

In the 1612 lawsuit in London of *Belott vs. Mountjoy* (see Chapter XIII, B *infra*), in which, as we shall see, Shakespeare himself appeared as a witness and signed his own deposition, he *had* to tell the court scrivener what his name was, and it is spelled "William Shakespeare." On that deposition he signed, as he always did, with an abbreviation, in that instance "Willm. Shakp." In the other depositions in that case (all printed, with the original spelling, in *Chambers,* Vol. II, pp. 90 et seq.), his name, which appears many times, is uniformly spelled "William Shakespeare" except for one "Mr. Shakspeare."

In the grant of his father's coat-of-arms it is spelled "Shakespeare" in the 1596 papers, and "Shakespere" in the 1599 papers.

In the will of his fellow-actor Augustine Phillips, leaving him as his "fellow" actor thirty shillings in gold, it is spelled "William Shakespeare," clearly revealing the name under which he was known to his fellow actors.

His own will describes him as "William Shackspeare." His daughter Susanna in a lawsuit after his death referred to him as "Willam Shakespeere." That Stratford monument spells the name "Shakspeare." On the tombstone of his wife and daughter it is spelled "Shakespeare." Instances could be greatly multiplied. (See *Chambers,* Vol. II, p. 371.)

Appleton Morgan, in his *The Shakespeare Myth,* p. 170, lists all of the spellings of his father's name (which, of course, was also the son's) in the records of the Town Council of Stratford, where the father long held office. The name appears there 166 times, with fourteen variant spellings. Seventeen were Shaksper, spelled one way or another; all the remaining 149 were Shakespeare, or Shakspeare, spelled one way or another.

It was, of course, customary in Elizabethan times to spell all names several different ways. Sir Walter Raleigh sometimes spelled his own name "Ralegh;" others spelled it "Rawley," "Rahley" or "Rawlie." Christopher Marlowe's name was spelled "Marloe," "Marley," "Morley" or, in hyphenated form, "Mar-low." The Earl of Oxford at times signed his name as 'Oxenford."

B.

That He Was Never Referred to as a Writer in His Lifetime

The *American Bar Association Journal* of February, 1959, at page 145, makes this amazing statement:

> "During Shaksper's entire life, however, not one of his contemporaries ever referred to him personally as a writer."

Since a dozen or so of his contemporaries did in his lifetime refer to the beautiful writings of "William Shakespeare" (all collected and printed in *Chambers*, Vol. II, pp. 186 et seq.), that statement obviously called for explanation. Called on thus to explain, the *Journal* of November, 1959, at page 1224, said:

> "There are allusions in contemporary writings during Shaksper's lifetime to the Shakespearean works, and to a person who wrote them, without otherwise identifying him in any way."

In other words, since his contemporaries in referring in his lifetime to Shakespeare's beautiful writing failed to state that "By William Shakespeare we refer to the man from Stratford," the *Journal* thus actually advises the lawyers of America that those references were not necessarily to the Stratford man but could have been references to the "real" Shakespeare, the great unknown!

The writers who on a number of occasions in his lifetime praised the beautiful poems and plays of "William Shakespeare" included some temperamental and jealous people, and they would hardly have referred to him simply (as they did) as "William Shakespeare" if they were referring to a great unknown. Curiosity, at least, would have consumed them and caused them to say more—unless, of course, they were all in on the "plot" and were consciously furthering it, in order to deceive posterity.

True, no contemporary writer in thus praising "William Shakespeare" as a writer ever added "By William Shakespeare we mean the man from Stratford." So too in our day when we say "Mark Twain" we don't find it necessary to add "By Mark Twain we mean Samuel Clemens of Hannibal, Missouri." But that, today, is because but one Mark Twain is in the public eye. Further identification is unnecessary. So it was in Shakespeare's day. There was one Shakespeare in the public eye, namely Shakespeare the actor—and there was no other, at least not in the public eye. If some pretender were the actual author, the real "Shakespeare," he was at least securely hidden. The public did not know of him. How could the contemporary writers have been referring to *him?* Shakespeare the actor was the only one known to the public—making explanatory words unnecessary.

By the publication in 1593 and 1594 of his two lyric poems *Venus & Adonis* and *The Rape of Lucrece* the name "William Shakespeare" became famous more or less overnight in literary London. Each of those poems, in book form, was enormously popular, *Venus & Adonis* going eventually through thirty editions, *The Rape of Lucrece* eight. Then, in the late 1590s, as some of the plays got published bearing his name, and as he himself continued to act on the stage, his prominence increased.

No contemporary statement ever once suggested that in addition to this William Shakespeare in the public eye, on the stage, another one was somewhere hidden away. Hence references to "William Shakespeare" could only have been references to him—unless, indeed, the "plot" theory is accepted, with many, many people in on the secret, which none of them ever revealed.

Even so, even on its own terms, the *American Bar Association Journal* is wholly inaccurate in stating that no contemporary writer referred to him as a writer while he was alive. In at least one instance, a very famous one quoted in many books, reference is made to "Shakespeare" with clear identification of "Shakespeare" as both playwright and actor,—and only the man from Stratford was both playwright and actor. Not one of the pretenders was an actor.

This reference, extremely well known and many times quoted over the years, appears in two plays put on by the young students at St. John's College, Cambridge, in 1598 and 1602, by which latter date Shakespeare had reached his thirty-eighth birthday. The plays were named *The Pilgrimage to Parnassus* and *The Return from Parnassus*.

These undergraduates were of the gentry and nobility, famous for being youthful, exuberant, smart and witty—and thoroughly worldly-wise. No fraudulent poseur could have fooled *them* for long. Here in these two plays which they wrote and produced they tell us that Shakespeare was both playwright and actor—and was so much their favorite they would keep his picture in their "study at the courte."

In *The Pilgrimage to Parnassus*, performed in 1598, one character in the play was "sick-thoughted Gullio," apparently a neurotic, who was in love and wanted help from another character, Ingenioso, in writing some poetry to woo his lady. Ingenioso, thus approached, said "We shall have nothing but pure Shakespeare"—and asks in what "vayne" he should compose these amatory verses. Then, from Gullio, comes some pure college-boy humor (*Chambers*, Vol. II, p. 200):

> "Not in a vaine veine (prettie, i' faith!): Make me them in two or three divers vayns, in Chaucer's, Gower's and Spencer's and Mr. Shakespeare's."

He thereupon quotes a few lines from Shakespeare's *Venus & Adonis* and then goes on to say:

> "O Sweet Mr. Shakespeare! I'll have his picture in my study at the courte."

Whether this means that by 1598 pictures of Shakespeare were available we do not know; certainly none has survived. But having here revealed that Shakespeare was their favorite poet they went on, in the second play, to state that he was both playwright and actor.

In that second play, *The Return From Parnassus*, performed in 1602, two characters in the play have the names of two of Shakespeare's fellow actors, Kempe and Burbage, and "Kempe" has these lines (*Chambers*, Vol. II, p. 201):

> "Few of the university men pen plaies well, they smell too much of that writer *Ovid*, and that that writer *Metamorphosis*, and talke too much of *Proserpina* and *Juppiter*. Why here's our fellow *Shakespeare* puts them all downe, I and Ben *Jonson* too. O that *Ben Jonson* is a pestilent fellow, he brought up *Horace* giving the Poets a pill, but our fellow *Shakespeare* hath given him a purge that made him beray his credit."

The well-known "playwrights' war" was going on at about this time, with the various playwrights taking cracks at each other, and this is an obvious reference to it.

Here we see the young law students refer to Shakespeare as Kempe's "fellow" actor, and also as the one who puts all the university playwrights, "and Ben Jonson too," down. Since there was no other playwright of consequence at the time who was also an actor (and certainly not one of the pretenders, be he Oxford, Bacon, Marlowe or whoever, was ever an actor), this is necessarily a reference to the man from Stratford.

Also, as we have seen, Francis Beaumont in 1615, while Shakespeare of Stratford was still alive, wrote his recently discovered verse letter to Ben Jonson in which he referred to "Shakespeare" as having gone far without "schollershippe" but "by the dimme light of Nature." By no stretch of the imagination could this have been a reference to any of the pretenders, only to the "upstart Crow" from Stratford.

Thus we see that in his lifetime Shakespeare of Stratford *was* referred to by his contemporaries as the author, and the *American Bar Association Journal's* statements to the contrary are simply untrue.

C.

That the Stratford Man Had Insufficient Education to have been The Author

Here we see soil in which the "impossibility" theory has some of its most tenacious roots—he lacked the necessary education. In fact, some of our anti-Stratfordian friends become rather extreme and express doubt that he could even read. (See Looney, *"Shakespeare" Identified*, p. 23.) Since we know documentarily that at least two of his long-time friends and relatives wrote him letters, one being Richard Quiney who grew up with him in Stratford and whose son married Shakespeare's daughter, and the other being Thomas Greene, his cousin, and since they obviously would not have written him letters he couldn't read, that view can be passed by in safety.

No one knows the education the Stratford man had. It cannot be proved documentarily that he ever went to school at all, for all Stratford pupil lists of those days have been lost. For that reason it cannot be proved documentarily that *any* Stratford youth of his day went to school. However, it is documentarily known that in his day there was in Stratford a free school.

In any event, it is a wholly pointless argument. For "William Shakespeare," no matter who he was or whether he was or was not educated, had a mind that created several thousand words in the English language, and showed the deepest insight into human nature of any writer in history. To say that such a mind could not have functioned without first having gone to college is to make a most extraordinary statement.

D.

That He Was a "Grain Dealer"

This, for some reason, is an item that our anti-Stratfordian friends cling tenaciously to. Thus Looney (*"Shakespeare" Identified*, p. 49) tells us that in Stratford he turned "his attention to houses, land, malt and money," and (p. 36) devoted himself "to houses, lands, orchards, money and malt;" the *American Bar Association Journal*, September, 1959, p. 941, that he was a "profiteer in grain;" and the Ogburns (*"Shakespeare" The Real Man Behind the Name*, p. 192) that he was a "well-known local grain-dealer."

The thought seems to be that if the Stratford man put his mind on such mundane matters he could not have been the great poet. Thus it helps to support the "impossibility" theory.

Without here considering the soundness of that argument, it is sufficient to reveal that to support their charge that he was a "grain-dealer" there are two, and only two, instances showing he invested in grain, two instances over a period of twenty years.

The entire evidence on this frequently mentioned point is documented by Sir Edmund Chambers (*Chambers*, Vol. II, pp. 99 et seq.).

The summers of 1595, 1596 and 1597, when Shakespeare was in London, had been "wet summers," resulting in grain shortage. Many Stratford citizens (but not Shakespeare) were reported in 1597 as "great corn-buyers" evading the law as they bought and hoarded grain, waiting for a price rise. In 1598 the government survey dated February 4 (see *Chambers,* Vol. II, p. 99), for the first and only time, showed "Wm. Shackspeare" as one of these. He had "ten quarters" (about eighty bushels) in his barn, an amount above the legal limit. However, practically every leading citizen of Stratford was doing the same, at least twelve being revealed by the survey of February 4 as hoarding more than he was. A better harvest in 1599 relieved the situation, and nothing more was heard of it.

Then in July, 1604, the Stratford Court of Records reveals that "Willielmus Shakspere" brought suit against one Philip Rogers for the sum of one pound fifteen shillings, the purchase price of some malt he had sold him. Since we have documentary proof, his own sworn testimony in the *Belott-Mountjoy* litigation (see Chapter XIII, B), that Shakespeare was then living in London, his Stratford lawyer must have handled this little collection claim for him.

Over his entire life there is not one further shred of evidence that he dealt in grain.

E.

That He Could Not Have Been the Author Because No Record Exists of His Ever Having Received Payment for the Plays

This is in part correct—i.e., that there is no known record of any payment to him for the plays.

The *American Bar Association Journal* articles seek to make much of this. In its issue of November, 1959, page 1163, the

Journal correctly states that Philip Henslowe, a London theatrical producer of the day, kept records (known as *Henslowe's Diary*) in which he recorded payments he made for plays, records which "cover the period 1591 to 1609." They show payments to Ben Jonson, Dekker, Webster and other playwrights, but never one to "Shaksper" or Shakespeare.

But that fact is wholly uninformative, for *Henslowe's Diary*, as has frequently been pointed out, contains not *one* entry of *any* payment to *any* playwright prior to 1597. (Robertson, *The Baconian Heresy*, p. 570.) By that year, in fact by several years prior thereto, the Chamberlain's Company, of which Shakespeare was permanent member from 1595 on, had permanently ceased using Henslowe or his theatres. They had and were using a theatre of their own.

From at least 1595 till at least 1608, as the documents show, Shakespeare was a full-time member, and for most of those years part owner, of the Chamberlain's Company. That Company alone produced all of his plays throughout those years. Whether his fellow actors paid him directly for the plays, or paid him via a larger cut in the gate-receipts, no one knows; but as a substantial co-owner of the Company he was receiving his reward. Since plays rarely sold for more than ten pounds he would have been foolish not to have taken his reward via the gate-receipts, which continued for years.

F.

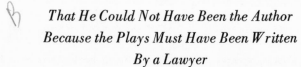

That He Could Not Have Been the Author Because the Plays Must Have Been Written By a Lawyer

This old chestnut has been exploded many times in many books, but our anti-Stratfordian friends cling stubbornly to it.

To bolster their argument they frequently cite Lord Campbell, successively Lord Chief Justice and Lord Chancellor of England, as agreeing with that theory, but on that point the documented record shows them to be wrong.

Lord Campbell was brought into the picture by one J. Payne Collier in 1859. Mr. Collier was one of those "Bardolators" who eagerly wanted to prove how vast was the knowledge of his hero from Stratford, and in 1859 he dreamt up the idea that since legal terms appear in the plays Shakespeare must have been a lawyer. In 1859 he wrote to Lord Campbell and suggested the possibility.

Obviously interested, Lord Campbell promptly wrote a disquisition on the subject entitled *Shakespeare's Legal Acquirements Considered,* and in it said that he considered Shakespeare's legal knowledge unquestionably great and advised the eager Mr. Collier that "there is nothing conclusive against you."

However, Lord Campbell then said:

"Still, I warn you that I myself remain sceptical."

The trouble with Mr. J. Payne Collier, and with the Lord Chief Justice too, for that matter, was that they were grossly ignorant of Elizabethan literature as a whole. For, as many scholars in that field have many times pointed out, almost every playwright of the era, and writers in other fields too, made much use of legal phraseology—many to a far greater extent than did Shakespeare. It has become a cliché among scholars of Elizabethan literature that if use of legal phraseology proves that the author of the Shakespearean plays was a lawyer, then on precisely the same line of reasoning almost the whole of Elizabethan literature must have been written by lawyers. (See H. N. Gibson's *The Shakespeare Claimants,* p. 50.)

All of this is quite crushingly demonstrated by Mr. J. M. Robertson in his *The Baconian Heresy.* There Mr. Robertson, a great scholar of Elizabethan literature and himself with five years' experience in a lawyer's office, devotes over one hundred pages to listing citation after citation from the Shakespearean plays (on which our anti-Stratfordian friends rely), following each with citation after citation from many other contemporary authors using identical or equally legalistic language.

Others besides Mr. Robertson have done the same. Paul Clarkson and Clyde Warren, in their *The Law of Property in Shakespeare and the Elizabethan Drama*, state their conclusion as follows:

> ". . . about half of Shakespeare's fellows employed on the average more legalisms than he did—some of them a great many more. For example the sixteen plays of Ben Jonson . . . have a total of over five hundred references from all fields of law. This surpasses Shakespeare's total from more than twice as many plays."

The Elizabethan age was a litigious era, with the general public widely familiar with legal phraseology. The very fact that so many playwrights used legal terms proves that the audiences must have been familiar with them too—for otherwise why would the playwrights have used them? As well use *Chinese* words on the stage, if the audience didn't know the meaning.

G.

That the Disappearance of All Manuscripts of the Plays Proves an Attempt to Conceal the Authorship

Of all the Shakespearean plays, not one original manuscript has ever been found. Highly suspicious, this, our anti-Stratfordian friends would have us believe. It proves, they tell us, that the "grand possessors" of the manuscripts, those hidden conspirators, permitted the printers to publish them but took the manuscripts back and either destroyed or hid them, to keep the hand-writing (of Bacon, Oxford, Marlowe or whoever) from being revealed.

The only trouble with that argument, a trouble that totally destroys it, is that *every* play manuscript, no matter by whom, if published prior to 1700, has totally disappeared. In those days they didn't regard manuscripts as important, once put into print. Paper was scarce, and the manuscripts were used as scrap paper. As the Folger Shakespeare Library puts it, in its pamphlet *The Authorship of Shakespeare*, page 29:

> "Of all the hundreds of plays put in print up to 1700, there is not one surviving example of a manuscript that went through a print shop."

Naturally, along with all the others, the Shakespearean manuscripts disappeared too.

H.

That the Dating of the Plays Should Be Pushed Back Ten Years

Since Oxford died in 1604 and Shakespearean plays nevertheless kept coming out for the next several years, some of our anti-Stratfordian friends find this highly embarrassing. Accordingly they put forth arguments to show that the plays must all have been written some ten years earlier than scholars believe and were released one by one, some after Oxford's death.

This argument reveals ignorance of Elizabethan literature as a whole, for the dates given by scholars to the writing of the plays fit perfectly with the chronology of the development of Elizabethan drama.

Was Shakespeare Shakespeare?

To sustain their argument, our anti-Stratfordian friends would have us believe that Shakespeare *preceded* Marlowe, Greene, Kyd, Peele and others whose writings clearly influenced the early writing of Shakespeare. Instead of their influencing Shakespeare, they contend, Shakespeare influenced them.

Such a contention, all scholars agree, would scramble Elizabethan literature and show a total jumble instead of the clear and orderly development that existed—where, from 1585 through Shakespeare's life-time, the drama grew steadily from phase to higher phase of play-writing, with each improved development clearly dateable, culminating in the Shakespearean plays.

Also, in 1598 Meres listed the known works of Shakespeare in his *Palladis Tamia,* giving eleven out of the thirteen plays now known to have then been written. If the schedule is set back ten years, to accommodate the Oxfordians, it would mean that by 1598, in addition to the plays Meres lists there would also have been written by then (but strangely omitted by Meres), *King Lear, Antony & Cleopatra, Hamlet, Macbeth, Twelfth Night* and *Measure for Measure*— indeed an odd bit of oversight on the part of Mr. Meres.

I.

That He Could Not Have Been the Author Because He Made No Mention of the Plays in His Will

Our anti-Stratfordian friends attempt to make much of this point. The *American Bar Association Journal* (November, 1959, page 1163) puts it this way:

"When Shaksper died, twenty of the Shakespeare plays were

unpublished and thus protected, yet the will made no reference to such valuable property."

Had the Stratford man been the author, so the argument goes, he would surely have mentioned the plays in his will and bequeathed his rights in them to his heirs.

But what our anti-Stratfordian friends fail to tell us is: *What* rights?

Shakespeare no longer had any rights in or to the plays. They no longer belonged to him, but to his old acting group, the King's Men, to whom he had sold or conveyed them. This is clearly revealed by certain events in 1619.

In that year 1619 two London publishers, Pavier and Jaggard, set about the publication of some of the Shakespearean plays plus two plays *(Sir John Oldcastle* and *A Yorkshire Tragedy)* not by Shakespeare, but which their book would ascribe to him.

The King's Men intervened.

On May 3, 1619, a letter was addressed by the Lord Chamberlain to the Stationers' Company (which, under Privy Council, had dictatorial jurisdiction over such matters), directing that none of the King's Men's plays should be printed without the consent of the actors. Then followed the order by the Stationers' Company, also dated May 3, 1619, ordering:

"That no playes that his Maiesties players do play shalbe printed without the consent of somme of them." (Hinman, *The Printing and Proof-Reading of the First Folio of Shakespeare*, Vol. I, p. 27.)

In his letter of May 3, 1619, directing the Stationers' Company to issue the above order the Lord Chamberlain had said (*Chambers*, Vol. I, p. 136):

"I am informed that some copies of playes belonging to the King

and queene's servants, the players, and purchased by them at
dear rates, having been lately stollen or gotten from them by in-
direct means, are now attempted to be printed . . ."

The order seems to have led to some confusion, resulting in
Pavier and Jaggard surreptitiously printing their book and
fraudulently antedating it.

The entire story is set forth by Sir Edmund Chambers (*Chambers*, Vol. I, pp. 133-137). It is intriguing to note there that the
Lord Chamberlain said that the plays had been *"purchased by
them* (i.e. the actors) *at dear rates."*

In commenting on all this, Charlton Hinman in his mon-
umental work, *The Printing and Proof-Reading of the First
Folio of Shakespeare,* says (Vol. I, p. 28):

"In view of the Stationers' Company order of 3 May 1619
(*Court-Book C*, p. 110) requiring that no King's Company play
be printed without the players' consent, Thomas Walkley's publication of *Othello* some time in 1622 inevitably raises certain
questions."

In other words, despite the Stationers' Company's order, an
occasional bootlegged publication does seem to have appeared.
But that the plays belonged to the King's Men and not to Shakespeare of Stratford is crystal clear. He had no rights in them he
could have bequeathed to his heirs.

XII

That Impossible Elizabethan "Plot" to Hide the True Authorship

THIS theory, that there was a great "plot" by the insiders to hide the true authorship, is essential to the claims of every pretender. Only with this theory can the overwhelming documented evidence against them be brushed aside—hence, to a man our anti-Stratfordian friends cling to it, as indeed they are compelled to do.

Of the many theories they ask us to accept, surely this is the one that is most impossible of belief.

It is a "plot" that had to have been in existence at least as early as 1592 and had to have continued, through enormous complexities, till at least 1640. Literally hundreds of Elizabethans had to have been in on it—yet never once did any whisper, even any hint, of it leak out. There is no evidence whatsoever showing a plot. Still, insist our anti-Stratfordian friends, it existed.

A conspiracy, of course, has to have originated with someone, has to have orders for its enforcement issued by someone, and has to have someone continuously on the alert with power to enforce it. And above all, it has to have motive, if it is to be believable. On all these points our anti-Stratfordian friends not only are vague, they do not agree among themselves.

For example, the *American Bar Association Journal* at one point tells us that Queen Elizabeth herself began it all—originated it because some of the plays made "the foibles and sins of those at Court" look bad. It would therefore never do to let the general public learn that they had been written by an insider, one who knew what the Court was really like. Let the public believe that that ignorant man from Stratford wrote them!

Says the *Journal*, February, 1959, page 208, on this point:

> "In spite of her love of literature, the Queen could not ignore this hazard. We are told that at Burghley's instigation" (Burghley being her chief minister) "she herself enjoined anonymity upon Oxford as the price of his freedom to write as he chose."

If Bacon and not Oxford was the one doing the writing, it must have been on him that she clamped this injunction; similarly with Walsingham, if Marlowe was the writer.

Oxford (and the same goes for any other pretender) supposedly was writing the plays under the name "William Shakespeare" (for reasons that remain obscure), and the *Journal* goes on to tell us:

> "The argument is that Shaksper of Stratford took advantage of the official conspiracy of silence about Oxford's authorship, and used the resemblance of his name to insinuate his authorship, which Oxford was powerless to deny."

Thus we are told that by great coincidence Shakespeare of Stratford had identically the same name as the *nom-de-plume* Oxford happened to choose for himself, and seeing his chance he took it. Since Oxford (or any other pretender were he the author), had Queen Elizabeth to back him up, he was hardly "powerless" to prevent this. To have clamped silently down on

96

that presumptuous man from Stratford would have been so easy that failure to do so is surprising.

In any event, Queen Elizabeth died in 1603 and her successor King James loved the plays and highly honored the actors, including Shakespeare, all as we have seen. Yet throughout the years of his reign the "plot" not only continued but vastly increased in complexity—with still no breath of it leaking out. And after James came Charles who also loved the plays—yet on and on went the "plot."

To explain this the *Journal* at another point (May, 1960, p. 522) tells us that it wasn't only Queen Elizabeth who enjoined anonymity, it was the Earls of Derby, Pembroke, Oxford and Montgomery, and their wives.

In any event, the "plot" lasted many years. It had to have begun at least by 1592, when the hack writer Chettle was throttled for publishing *Groatsworth of Wit*. Then, as we have seen, in 1595 when Privy Council records reveal a payment to Shakespeare and two of his fellow actors for plays produced at Court, it is the "plot" that explains it away. So Chettle was in on it, as were those in charge of Privy Council records.

The actors all had to be in on it, for if their fellow actor Shakespeare was not the author he could not have fooled them. Then the *American Bar Association Journal*, September, 1959, page 995, informs us categorically that "all the writers knew Shakespeare's identity,"—and indeed they must have known, if the actor was a fraud, and must have been enjoined by those enforcing the "plot," for none of them ever breathed a whisper of the secret. And the writers who mentioned "Shakespeare" were quite numerous, and some had the reputation of being both jealous and hard to control. But one and all they remained silent on this point.

In 1598, as we have seen, Francis Meres, the one literary historian of the day, wrote in his *Palladis Tamia* about the beautiful poems and plays of Shakespeare, mentioning also that the

Earl of Oxford wrote comedies. But Meres, the *American Bar Association Journal* tells us (September, 1959, p. 994), was "commissioned" to write that way so as to keep the public fooled as to the authorship. So Meres, too, was in on the "plot."

Then in 1616 Ben Jonson brought out his *Works* and stated that Will. Shakespeare had acted in two of Jonson's plays. This, the "plot" theory tells us, Jonson did in order to pave the way for the fraudulent *First Folio*, which the great conspirators in London were planning to bring out seven years later, in 1623, as "William Shakespeare's." With this fraudulent act by Jonson in 1616 "an important step had now been taken with intent to deceive posterity." (*"Shakespeare," The Real Man Behind the Name*, pages 112-113.) So Ben Jonson too was in on the "plot."

From 1616 on, Jonson, the theory tells us, played a more and more fraudulent and complicated role in the "plot." By then, says the theory, Jonson had been hired by the great conspirators in London, whose identity is not completely clear, to go to some amazing extremes of deception. For in 1616 the great conspirators learned in some unexplained way that up in Stratford Shakespeare, shortly to die, was about to draw or had drawn his will. Odd that they should have found that out, but find it out they did. So they sent Jonson up to Stratford where he succeeded in getting bequests to the last remaining three of Shakespeare's old fellow actors criminally inserted in the will. Those bequests, the theory is, were thus fraudulently inserted to give a realistic touch when, seven years later, two of those three fellow actors were to bring out the *First Folio*, stating that the plays were by William Shakespeare, their fellow actor.

Amazing as all this is, the most amazing part is still to come—namely, that when his contemporaries, in or shortly after 1616, erected a monument to him in his church in Stratford, stating in words carved in stone that he it was who was the writer, it was fraudulent and was done merely to deceive the public. That statue *too* was part of the "plot"!

Then came 1623 when the *First Folio* came out. In it several eminent writers of the day, as well as the last surviving two of his old fellow actors, stated unequivocally that the plays were written by Shakespeare of Stratford, the actor. But they, the theory assures us, were all in on the "plot", and were all giving false testimony.

Finally, in 1640, an edition of *The Poems of Will. Shake-Speare, Gent.* was published, with further testimony by other eminent contemporaries. But these contained "clues regarding the identity of the author deliberately pointing away from Shaksper of Stratford . . . We are led to conclude that someone is tipping us off." (*"Shakespeare," The Real Man Behind The Name*, p. 152.)

Who enforced this great conspiracy in all the years from 1592 to 1640, so that no whisper of it leaked out, our anti-Stratfordian friends do not tell us. Nor do they tell us what conceivably could have been the motive. Elizabeth died in 1603, Oxford in 1604, Shakespeare in 1616, Bacon in 1626. Marlowe had been officially dead since 1593. The plays had (with the possible exception of *Troilus & Cressida*) been many times produced for the public over many years, had been royal favorites, after Elizabeth's death, with both James and Charles. Also they had, by 1623, all been published, a number of them prior thereto. Just why were the great conspirators (identity not clear) so pathologically afraid to let Oxford's or Bacon's or Marlowe's authorship become publicly known? What harm could it have done at *that* late date?

Yet this theory of a great "plot" is utterly essential to the claim of every pretender. Only with this "plot" theory, totally without evidentiary support, can the documented evidence that overwhelms them be brushed aside.

The *American Bar Association Journal*, May, 1960, page 522, puts it all this way:

"By holding back the publication of the plays until Oxford had been dead eighteen years and paying Ben Jonson, Heminge and Condell a total of some two hundred pounds, slipping a few entries into the Stratford man's will, and erecting a monument in Stratford Church with a craftily worded inscription upon it to mystify the populace, the Earls of Derby, Pembroke, Oxford and Montgomery and their wives put over a hoax which has lasted three hundred and fifty years . . ."

In asking us to forget for awhile the documented evidence and in its place accept the unsupported "plot" theory, our anti-Stratfordian friends do seem to have reached their finest hour of self-delusion.

XIII

Newly Discovered Facts That Reveal Indirect Bearing on the Authorship Question

---

A.

His Close Friendship With the Wits of the Mermaid Tavern

Famous among the gayest of the revelries of Elizabethan days were the monthly occasions when London's leading literary wits assembled at the Mermaid Tavern and strove, with some help from the Mermaid's wine, to out-do one another in witty forays.

Those gatherings have been immortalized by Tom Coryate who coined the word "Sirenaicks" from "Siren"—hence "Mermaid." The group, he tells us, included Ben Jonson, John Donne, Christopher Brooke and other "right generous, jovial and mercurial Sireniacks," who met, he said, on the first Friday of each month, for wit and revelry.

Other writers of the day support Coryate's statement that the occasions were beyond question gay. Frank Beaumont, the playwright, wrote to Ben Jonson anent these gatherings (Hotson, *Shakespeare's Sonnets Dated,* p. 87):

> "What things have we seen
> Done at the Mermaid, heard words that have been
> So nimble, and so full of subtill flame,
> As if that every one from whence they came
> Had meant to put his whole wit in a jest,
> And had resolv'd to live a foole, the rest
> Of his dull life."

In his *Epigrams* Ben Jonson revealed his own favoritism for the Mermaid, saying (same, p. 78):

> "That which most doth take my muse and me
> Is a pure cup of rich Canary wine,
> Which is the Mermaid's now, but shall be mine."

That Ben took this attitude on more than one occasion is revealed in this friendly gibe at him:

> "That such thy draught was, and so great thy thirst,
> That all thy plays were drawn at the Mermaid first."

> (same, p. 78.)

It has often been wondered whether Shakespeare of Stratford joined in those revels. No document expressly stating that he did has ever, as yet, been found. Furthermore, he was apparently not a hard-drinking man, and there is at least some indication that he was apt to shy away from such goings on, for, many years after his death, John Aubrey wrote in 1681 that he "was not a company keeper" and "wouldn't be debauched." ("Debauched" does seem a rather harsh word for what those boys at the Mermaid were doing.)

However, that he had a tolerance of hard drinking in others, seems clear. Falstaff alone, written with such profound affection, shows that he did not look upon hard-drinking roisterers with any grim Puritan eye.

And now newly discovered documentary evidence, first published for us in the 1940s, shows that whether he did or did not drink frequently at the Mermaid Tavern (and the probability would seem to be that he did not), he associated with his gay contemporaries there on terms of close intimacy and affectionate friendship. Clearly he was one of their circle.

This evidence was discovered by Dr. Leslie Hotson, and was published, with Dr. Hotson's usual impeccable documentation, in the 1940s in his *Shakespeare's Sonnets Dated*, pp. 76 et seq.

Its discovery stems from Shakespeare's purchase, in 1613, of the Gate-House in Blackfriars, described in *Chambers*, Vol. II, pp. 154 et seq. On March 10 of that year Shakespeare (described in the deed as "William Shakespeare of Stratford upon Avon in the Countie of Warwick gentleman") bought the Gate-House for one hundred and forty pounds. The purchase deed was drawn in duplicate originals, one of which is now in the Folger Library in Washington, the only document in America known once to have been held in Shakespeare's hands. For five dollars a photostatic copy can be obtained from the Folger by mail.

The deed is in actuality a deed of trust, with title vesting in three named trustees, thus keeping wife Anne from getting a dower interest, which may have been his purpose. But it is not the purchase that especially interests us, it is those three trustees. They are named in the deed:

"William Johnson, citizein and Vintener of London, John Jackson and John Hemmyng of London gentlemen." (*Chambers*, Vol. II, p. 154)

"John Hemmyng" is, of course, Shakespeare's long-time friend and fellow actor John Heminges of the Chamberlain's

Company—King's Men group, who ten years later was to bring out the *First Folio*.

It is the other two trustees that now, under Dr. Hotson's research, tell us so revealing a story.

Dr. Hotson sets it all forth, thoroughly documented, in two chapters and Appendix A in his *Shakespeare's Sonnets Dated*.

First, there was "William Johnson, citizein and Vintener of London." With that word "Vintener" as his opening clue Dr. Hotson found in Vintners' Hall, London, the records of the "Worshipped Company of Vintners." There it was documentarily revealed that one William Johnson served nine years, beginning 1591 as apprentice to William Williamson, owner of the Mermaid Tavern, and in 1603 bought the Tavern for 1848 pounds, continuing as owner through 1616. The only remaining question was: Was this the same William Johnson who served as Shakespeare's trustee?

By long research through the vast collection of Town Depositions in Chancery, Dr. Hotson eventually found a deposition dated October 25, 1614, signed by this William Johnson who owned the Mermaid Tavern; and by actual comparison of signatures showed that he and Shakespeare's trustee were one and the same man. It is careful, painstaking research like that that is bringing to us the incontrovertible story of the authorship. Dreamt-up theories are not involved.

Then, with equally painstaking and careful research Dr. Hotson reveals that the other trustee "John Jackson, Gentleman," was one of the literary wits who added materially to the Mermaid's monthly revels. He gives us, in his *Shakespeare's Sonnets Dated*, speciments of Mr. Jackson's contributions to the gaiety of those occasions.

Dr. Hotson then takes us further. The deed of trust for the Gate-House purchase was acknowledged before Gregory Donhault, Esquire, "Master in Chancery." With that as his clue Dr. Hotson, indefatigable as always, searched out Donhault's will, in the hope of finding more. The will, he discovered, had been made April 1, 1614, just one year after the Gate House purchase and shortly before Donhault died. In the will Donhault left to this same John Jackson, in terms showing strong personal friendship, the large sum of two hundred pounds; left also one hundred pounds to found a scholarship at Pembroke College; and in the will referred to a diamond ring given him by the Countess of Pembroke herself. From this it is clear that Donhault, close friend of Shakespeare's trustee John Jackson, was also close to the house of Pembroke. The Earl of Pembroke was one of the two to whom the *First Folio* was later dedicated. If there had been any shenanigans going on, with a fraudulent Shakespeare claiming to have written plays that were not his, with Pembroke and his wife involved in hiding the authorship, as our anti-Stratfordian friends would have us believe, this Donhault, "Master in Chancery," would probably have known of it via Pembroke—and could have warned his friend Jackson not to serve as trustee for so fraudulent a fellow. Instead, Donhault took the acknowledgment.

Certainly this latter information could not be called evidence of the authorship; but equally certainly it throws light on the caliber of the men who were then willingly serving Shakespeare of Stratford as he put his property in trustee hands. They were no fly-by-night people; they were high and important in the realm—and were intimately connected with the wits of the Mermaid Tavern.

Nor were those trustees in any sense dummies, with no duties to perform. They were putting themselves out for Shakespeare of Stratford, and could have been doing so for no reason whatsoever except friendship. Not only did they thus take on the duties of trustees holding property; in 1618, two years after Shakespeare's death, they took court action to transfer the Gate House so that it came to Shakespeare's daughter, Susanna, to carry out the terms of Shakespeare's will.

Thus it is that we see Shakespeare of Stratford associating on terms of friendly intimacy with the host of the Mermaid Tavern and with at least one of the wits who made revelry there. Had he been, as our anti-Stratfordian friends would have us believe, merely a small-minded businessman, intent only on money, real-estate and the like, he could never have joined that circle.

B.

William Shakespeare Himself Plays The Role of Cupid in a Real-Life Romance

This thoroughly documented event occurred in 1604. Not until 1910, however, were the original documents that reveal it discovered, all printed in *Chambers*, Vol. II, pages 90 et seq.; and not until the 1940s were the supplementary documents, completely rounding out the story, published, in Dr. Leslie Hotson's *Shakespeare's Sonnets Dated*.

In that year 1604 Shakespeare, as these documents reveal, was living as a lodger in the home of one Christopher Mountjoy, on Silver Street, in London, and had been living there since 1602. Mountjoy the landlord was an artist of high caliber, a maker of ladies' head-dresses of "Venice gold and silver thread" sometimes "garnished with rubies," and one of his regular clients was none other than the Queen of England herself, Anne, the wife of James.

In that home on Silver Street in those years between 1602 and 1604 Mountjoy had living with him an apprentice, a young man named Stephen Belott. Also living in the house was a daughter of marriageable age, Mary Mountjoy.

As might be expected, a romance blossomed between the apprentice and the daughter—but it did not proceed straight to the altar at a pace fast enough to satisfy Mrs. Mountjoy, Mary's mother.

Taking things into her own hands, as mothers have been known to do from time to time, Mrs. Mountjoy turned to her paying lodger, William Shakespeare himself, and enrolled him in her scheme. As Shakespeare later put it in his sworn and signed deposition, Mrs. Mountjoy "did sollicitt and entreat" him "to move and perswade" the young apprentice Belott "to effect the said marriage, and accordingly this deponent (i.e. William Shakespeare) did move and perswade" Belott "thereunto."

Shakespeare, thus "sollicitted" and, as always a practical man, approached the matter from a practical as well as a romantic point of view. He mentioned not only love, he mentioned dowry too. The dowry argument may or may not have been the clincher, but it is to the dowry that we are indebted for the entire story. For once daughter Mary was safely married, old man Mountjoy welched on his dowry promise, and in 1612 son-in-law Belott sued him for same. It is from the records of that lawsuit that we now have the facts.

The marriage took place on November 19, 1604, by which time, his deposition reveals, Shakespeare had been lodging there for two years; and in his deposition he tells us that preceding the marriage the family "had amongeste themselves manye conferences about there marriage which (afterwards) was consummated and solempnized." From his testimony one gets the impression that Shakespeare was definitely a member of the family circle.

It was not until 1612, eight years later, that son-in-law Belott finally brought suit, and by then Shakespeare couldn't remember just what dowry had been promised. Belott said sixty pounds, plus two hundred pounds more by will, but as to that Shakespeare deposed, in not un-Shakespearean language, that he "rememberethe not."

The case (*Chambers,* Vol. II, p. 95) was referred "for arbitration to the overseers and elders of the French Church in London," who "awarded Belott 20 nobles which Mountjoy had not paid a year later."

Apparently by that year 1612 the bloom on the romance between Belott and Mary had somewhat worn off, to say nothing of that between father-in-law Mountjoy and his wife, for the love-life of both men was deemed "scandalous" by the Church. Father-in-law was revealed as having gone to the extreme of actually keeping a mistress—a fact somewhat irrelevant to the dowry point, but enabling the church to criticize both parties quite sharply.

The *American Bar Association Journal,* in one of its articles, voices disapproval too, stating that the court found both men "to be low characters"—not the sort, the *Journal* author seems to feel, a great poet would have as friends.

On that latter point, however, Dr. Leslie Hotson comes to Shakespeare's complete rescue with thorough research scholarship, beautifully documented. He sets forth his findings at full length in his *Shakespeare's Sonnets Dated,* pages 174 et seq. Christopher Mountjoy was London's leading maker of ladies' head-dresses, "marvelous confections of gold, pearl and precious stones," in that field "an artist and craftsman, a kind of lesser Benvenuto Cellini, the kind of man Shakespeare would choose for a landlord." (p. 179.)

Not only that, Dr. Hotson goes on to reveal (always magnificently documented): "The gentry went to Mountjoy to adorn their ladies," as did Queen Anne herself. The accounts of Queen Anne for 1605 reveal payment to the Mountjoys of the large sum of £59 for the Queen's head-dresses. "Part of it," says Dr. Hotson, "was paid on November 17, 1604, two days before the wedding of her daughter Mary Mountjoy to Stephen Belott, the marriage Shakespeare had brought about."

Thus we see that, far from having retired to Stratford in 1597, as Looney and other of our anti-Stratfordian friends would have us believe, Shakespeare in those years between 1602 and 1604, was living in London in a household colorful and far from dull, with the gentry and the Queen herself involved, and was himself a part of the family milieu. Many references to Venice gold and silver thread, to beautiful ladies' head-dresses adorned with jewels, appear in several of Shakespeare's plays, all quoted by Dr. Hotson, and the source from which they sprang was clearly that home on Silver Street.

C.

Shakespeare, At Least Once, Lost His Temper and Lost It Violently

Ben Jonson, supported by all other writers of the day who mentioned him, called him "gentle" Shakespeare on more than one occasion; but that he was not wholly angelic is clearly indicated by the document Mr. Leslie Hotson discovered in 1931.

That document was a court order entered in the Controllment Rolls of the Queen's Bench in the form of a "writ of attachment" addressed to the Sheriff of Surrey. It was returnable November 29, 1596, and directed the Sheriff to protect the magistrate's deputy "William Wayte" from William "Shakspere," Francis Langley, theater-owner, and two unidentified ladies, "for fear of death."

A photograph of this intriguing document is on page 9 of Dr. Leslie Hotson's *Shakespeare Versus Shallow,* and in his book Dr. Hotson gives us the story, perfectly documented.

There, on page 9, Dr. Hotson says:

> "Shakespeare, hitherto known only as a poet and player affable and unobtrusive, now for the first time steps out of the dusty records of the past as protagonist in a turbulent scene of raw Elizabethan life. To be sure there is no actual fight to the

death, as in the cases of his fellow playwrights Watson, Marlowe, Jonson, Day and Portier; nevertheless this man Wayte swears that Shakespeare and these three other persons threatened him with death."

The *American Bar Association Journal,* February, 1959, page 144, deemed this document as worthy of no mention except that "he was put under a peace bond in 1596." Fortunately Dr. Hotson handled it with more creative research skill. As he shows us, thoroughly documented, this was no ordinary "breach of the peace," this was a determined attempt by Shakespeare to keep the magistrate's deputy, William Wayte, from closing down their theatre. Mr. Hotson gives us the full story in his *Shakespeare Versus Shallow,* and it is indeed an intriguing one, though having no bearing on the question of authorship. It does, however, to some extent reveal an unknown facet of Shakespeare's personality.

It happened in 1596. On July 22 of that year the Lord Mayor of London, perpetual enemy of the actors, succeeded in getting Privy Council (the Lord Chamberlain not being there to block him) to issue a decree prohibiting all plays throughout London.

This was a crippling blow to the actors, for it left them with no means of support unless they took to the provinces. However, there was one ray of light, and the actors of the Chamberlain's Company apparently decided to give it a try.

A wealthy London businessman named Francis Langley had just built a new theatre called the *Swan,* which was in Southwark across the Thames from the Lord Mayor's chief bailiwick. At that moment the *Swan* was available, and the actors' plan appears to have been to transfer their play-productions there— and from that safer distance to defy His Honor.

Unfortunately, however, in Southwark, where the *Swan* stood, lurked another menace the actors do not seem to have thought of. For the presiding magistrate in Southwark was a man named William Gardner who hated the Swan's owner, Mr. Francis

Langley, not only intensely but for a thoroughly understandable reason. For it so happened that a few months previously Mr. Langley had publicly called Magistrate Gardner "a false knave and a false perjured knave"— and had publicly offered to prove it. And, to make matters worse, the charge appears to have been true. For Magistrate Gardner promptly sued him for slander— but never let the case come to trial.

Magistrate Gardner was thus apparently in a mood to wreak vengeance on Mr. Langley, if only opportunity would offer— and then opportunity dropped squarely into his lap. Mr. Langley stepped into his jurisdiction and tried to open the *Swan*. Associated with him, in opening the *Swan*, appear to have been the actors of the Chamberlain's Company, including William Shakespeare.

Whether the actors actually moved into the *Swan*, or whether Magistrate Gardner blocked them, the documents do not tell us. But that the Magistrate set out to block them is apparent from the fact that the Magistrate's deputy who hurried in fear to the Sheriff for protection was Magistrate Gardner's own step-son and long-time stooge, William Wayte. It was against him that William Shakespeare lost his temper and apparently threatened to kill him.

The court thereupon issued the document discovered in 1931 by Dr. Hotson, the "writ of attachment" directing the Sheriff to protect "William Wayte" from "William Shakspere, Francis Langley, Dorothy Soer wife of John Soer, and Anna Lee, for fear of death."

Francis Langley owned the *Swan*; who the two ladies were has never been ascertained.

XIV

Those Pretenders

MANY times, in many books, the pretenders have been finished off, one and all. However, their supporters, totally convinced of the "impossibility" of the Stratford man's authorship, refuse to believe them dead. As the crushing evidence slaughters them, their supporters return each time to the field and breathe something resembling life back into them. It is far too intriguing a parlour game for any dedicated supporter to give up.

The claims of all of the pretenders, if our anti-Stratfordian friends will pardon the use of the word, are patently absurd. It is unthinkable that Shakespeare of Stratford could have worked intimately, as he did, with his fellow actors for over twenty years, fraudulently feeding them one by one thirty-six plays as his own, and never once have been denounced. It is equally unthinkable that his fellow actors, who could not have failed to know he was a fraud, would have taken him to their bosoms the way they did, working with him, leaving him at least once a bequest in their wills, serving him as trustee as Heminges did, when all the while his name grew and grew in fame throughout London— and then, after his death, have joined in perpetuating

112

his name in the *First Folio*. They were too human not to have been moved by jealousy.

Nor would the jealous playwrights have kept quiet—even collaborated in making him famous. Ben Jonson, so obviously a jealous man, could not have failed to expose the fraud—especially when, as late as 1641, his notebooks, to advise "posterity," were published.

It is the pretenders, not the orthodox Stratfordians, who ask us to believe something that "contravenes human experience."

Furthermore, there is not one shred of real evidence to support a single one of the pretenders—merely dreamt-up, unbelievable theories their supporters put forth. Mr. Gibson, in his *The Shakespeare Claimants*, p. 76, puts it this way as to where they get their material:

> "They blunder through Elizabethan history and literature, snatching at every little detail they think they can turn to account, and in their eagerness to swell the body of evidence for their own particular theory overlook the fact that these bits and pieces not only do not fit together, but often flatly contradict one another, and thus reduce their argument to chaos."

There Mr. Gibson puts his finger on the basic weakness of all anti-Stratfordians—they do not know Elizabethan literature as a whole, merely that portion of it that pleases and, in their opinions, supports them. But as Mr. Leslie Hotson has said (*Shakespeare's Sonnets Dated*, page 171): "we must know all the Elizabethans in order to know Shakespeare."

No scholar who has thoroughly known Elizabethan literature has ever once supported any pretender. The stock answer to that statement will be to name Sir George Greenwood, whose *The Shakespeare Problem Restated* (published in 1908) is still the classic anti-Stratfordian book. Sir George was a man of considerable forensic skill, and in his book he set forth approximately every theory and every argument on which our anti-

Stratfordian friends still rely today—no matter which pretender they back.

But Sir George, though well acquainted with the Shakespearean works, knew very little indeed about the rest of Elizabethan literature, and his many pages of quotations attempting to show that the true Shakespeare must have known law, classic literature and the like crumble into pointlessness when it is shown that the same material is to be found in great abundance in the works of many other Elizabethan writers. In that manner Mr. J. M. Robertson utterly slaughters *The Shakespeare Problem Restated* with his *The Baconian Heresy* published in 1913.

However, few of the real scholars pay any attention to the pretender claims, regarding them as nonsense—which is one of the reasons why anti-Stratfordianism continues in the public eye as it does.

A.

Sir Francis Bacon

Sir Francis Bacon, possibly England's greatest lawyer, was a man of enormous erudition whose life has been the subject of microscopic research and voluminous biography. Those who have thus researched his life, who above all others should know, have without exception denied that he was the author of the Shakespearean works. In fact, the suggestion seems to irritate them. His most recent biographer, Catherine Drinker Bowen, whose *Francis Bacon, the Temper of the Man,* was published in 1963, says on page 4 of her book that the claim that Bacon wrote Shakepeare's plays "is accompanied by smoke, necromancy, cryptography and the fanaticism of a religion. With it this book will not be concerned."

After Shakespeare of Stratford's death in 1616 no further new Shakespearean play ever appeared, though Sir Francis

114

lived healthily on for another ten years. That does not necessarily prove anything, but it does cast a doubt.

Also, in 1621-1623, when the *First Folio* was being pre-
pared for printing, Sir Francis was in London and very much
alive. All his life he had been careful to the degree of painful-
ness to edit out errors of proof-reading—yet there he sat and
let the *First Folio* come out abounding in such errors. Hardly
the Baconian custom, certainly.

The chief base on which Baconianism is founded is the argument that the author must have been a lawyer. But Elizabethan
literature abounds with legal terms and phrases, and the argument based on their use in Shakespeare's works is pointless.

As to his poetic ability, he published a metrical version of
the Psalms of David—which was where he should have used a
nom-de-plume, for one of the kindliest things said of it was that
it was "rather inferior."

His so-called "Promus," or as his biographer Spedding named
it, his *"Promus of Formularies and Elegancies,"* seems to stir
present-day Baconians most. It is currently in the British Museum.

It was first published in 1883. In its original form it consisted
of fifty folio sheets, all unnumbered, though for convenience,
when they were bound together with other Bacon papers, num-
bers were given to the pages.

The contents of the *Promus* consists of texts from the Bible,
metaphors, aphorisms, English, French, Spanish, Italian and
Latin proverbs, all taken from published collections, and a large
number of miscellaneous entries.

Many of the entries, or at least the thoughts they express, are
found in expanded form in some of the Shakespearean plays.
This, the Baconians claim, is proof that Bacon wrote the plays.

But the sources from which much of the *Promus* was com-
piled were as readily available to Shakespeare as to Bacon.
Furthermore, since it is impossible to date most of the *Promus*

pages, it could easily have been that Bacon actually took down some of the entries while personally in attendance at the plays.

The *Promus,* accordingly, cannot be regarded as proof, or even evidence, of anything.

B.

The Seventeenth Earl of Oxford

Of all the glittering personalities that surrounded the throne of England in Elizabethan days, few, if any, outshone Edward de Vere, the seventeenth Earl of Oxford. Highly educated, a warrior, a resplendent courtier demonstrably a favorite of the Queen, he was seventeenth in direct succession from a line of noble ancestors dating back to the days of William the Conqueror and earlier, quite possibly the number one peer of all England outside the royal family.

He was born in 1550, hence was older by fourteen years than Shakespeare of Stratford. A definite gift for poetic writing revealed itself early in him, and by the time he was twenty-six years old he had written, and circulated in manuscript form, some lovely short poems of which twenty-two have survived. Furthermore, in his thirties he demonstrated an interest in the theatre, supporting a company of youthful actors known as "Oxford's Boys," though how much he actually associated with them is not known. And he was twice reported as a writer of comedies for the stage, once by Puttenham in 1589, and again by Meres in 1598. It was in 1598 that Meres, in his *Palladis Tamia,* listed him, jointly with sixteen others including Shakespeare, as being "the best for Comedie amongst us." Not one of his comedies has survived.

So far as is known he stopped writing lyric poetry at or about the age of twenty-six, for nothing of a later date has been discovered. In or about 1592 he married his second wife and seems to have retired into almost complete seclusion, emerging into the public eye only a time or two thereafter, once in 1601 to sit as one of the judges in the trial of Essex. He died in 1604.

Says the *American Bar Association Journal* of him (May, 1960, page 521):

> ". . . nothing that we have from his pen was written after his twenty-sixth year. What was he writing during the rest of his life?
> "Answer: Everything known as that of William Shakespeare."

Unfortunately for that intriguing claim, not one shred of supporting evidence has ever been discovered, merely theory—plus what his supporters seem to consider "circumstantial evidence."

It was not until 1920 that Oxford's name was first put forward as a pretender. In that year his "discoverer," J. Thomas Looney, published his book *"Shakespeare" Identified,* and it is indeed impossible to read Looney's book and not be convinced at least of his sincere belief that he had at long last found the unknown "Shakespeare."

Looney arrived at his identification by a bit of strictly *a priori* reasoning. First, as does every anti-Stratfordian, he convinced himself that it was "impossible" for the plays and poems to have been written by that small-minded man from Stratford. To demonstrate this "impossibility" he informs his readers that the Stratford man's life is clearly divisible into three periods, namely, the early Stratford years, ending at least by 1592, when Greene's *Groatsworth* showed him to be in London; the middle or London years, ending (Looney tells us) in 1597, when he bought New Place in Stratford; and his final period, from 1597 to 1616, all of which he spent in Stratford engaging in small business deals and petty litigation.

That such a man could have written the Shakespearean works,

says Looney, "is impossible to believe," adding (page 49):

> ". . . it is the incredible that Stratfordianism has to face. . . . the common sense of mankind instinctively repudiates a moral contradiction as incredible. Such we hold is the belief in the Stratford man . . ."

He gives no other reason for his disbelief.

Next, having thus disposed of the Stratford man, or what he calls "the Stratford hypothesis," Looney set out to discover the hidden author. By a process of both analysis and synthesis, he examined the Shakespearean works to determine the "character and circumstances" of the genius who wrote them, whoever he was. Just what sort of man, he reasoned, do the works show the author to have been? Well, he concluded, he *must* have had *this* characteristic; he *must* have had *that* characteristic—and as he added these together, one by one, he began to have a clear idea in his own mind, so he tells us, of what sort of man the still unknown author must have been.

His conclusion was that the unknown author *must* have been a man with the following characteristics (p. 92):

"1. A mature man of recognized genius.
2. Apparently eccentric and mysterious.
3. Of intense sensibility—a man apart.
4. Unconventional.
5. Not adequately appreciated.
6. Of pronounced and known literary tastes.
7. A lyric poet of recognized talent.
8. Of superior education—classical—the
   habitual associate of educated people."

He then reasoned further with himself, and concluded that the following additional items were essential for a complete synthesis (p. 103):

"1. A man with Feudal connections.
~ 2. A member of the higher aristocracy.
3. Connected with Lancastrian supporters.
4. An enthusiast for Italy.
5. A follower of sport (including falconry).
6. A lover of music.
7. Loose and improvident in money matters.
8. Doubtful and somewhat conflicting in his attitude to women.
9. Of probably Catholic leanings, but touched with scepticism."

Having thus created his synthesized man, Looney's "next step was to proceed to search for him." To do this, he tells us, he turned with a completely open mind "to the Elizabethan lyric poets."

Since the unknown "Shakespeare" had stated that *Venus and Adonis* was the "first heir" of his invention, Looney turned first to that poem. Having familiarized himself with the stanza forms of *Venus and Adonis,* he went through "an anthology of six-teenth century poetry" looking for another poem with the same stanza form. "I was left ultimately" he tells us, "with only one"—a poem by Oxford beginning:

"If women could be fair and yet not fond."

So totally was Looney convinced that his poem revealed that the true author of the Shakespearean works was Oxford, that he quotes the poem in full "because of its importance to the history of English literature." Clearly he regarded himself as the Christopher Columbus of the great authorship search, and clearly he expected disciples to follow after him, for he said (p. 12):

". . . much remains to be done before the Stratford hypothesis will be sufficiently moribund to be disregarded."

119

He did not, of course, stop with that poem, but went on to tell how Oxford had all of the qualifications; and he cited many instances of Oxford's life which he claimed were mirrored in the plays and the *Sonnets.*

He admits his great "obligations" to Sir George Greenwood, and quite obviously he had been studying Greenwood's *The Shakespeare Problem Restated,* for he comes up with many of Sir George's arguments, and even goes so far, on page 37, as to refer to Shakespeare's Stratford monument as "mysterious," failing, however, to tell us why it was "mysterious." Also, in keeping with sound anti-Stratfordian practice, he fails even to mention Robertson's *The Baconian Heresy,* which doesn't merely puncture *The Shakespeare Problem Restated* but slaughters it.

He had considerable difficulty, naturally enough, in explaining why Oxford (and for generations thereafter Oxford's family) was so afraid that the news that he was the author might leak out. Finally he more or less gave up on that tough point, saying on page 46, "inability to fathom motives cannot be put in as an argument against the evidence of a fact," and on page 47, "we may . . . be quite unable to offer a satisfactory explanation." In fact, he goes so far (page 174) as to say that Oxford obviously wanted to remain anonymous and it is not up to us to ask why. "We may, if we wish, question the sufficiency or reasonableness of the motive. That, however, is his business, not ours."

Then, on page 176, he does say that " the role of dramatic author would have been completely fatal to any chances he may have had" to retrieve Oxford's financial position, which was in a tangle. And he tries to cover up another glaring fact which no Oxfordian can ever explain away, namely, that long after Oxford's death, as his widow and his son, the eighteenth Earl, struggled to recover "the prestige which had been lost," not once did they then at that late date claim that the seventeenth Earl had written the greatest literature in England's history. Such a claim, if they could substantiate it, would probably have done more to rehabilitate the family than anything they could have done, but they made no such claim. To have done so, says Looney, "would hardly have been in harmony with their general policy." "Motives," he adds, on page 177, "are sometimes altogether impenetrable."

Certainly one glaring weakness of Looney's reasoning springs from his lack of knowledge of facts about Shakespeare of Stratford, facts that had already been published by 1920, when Looney published his book. The strongest argument with which he convinced himself that for the Stratford man to have been the author was "impossible" is his claim that by 1597 Shakespeare had retired permanently to Stratford, bribed to do so, Looney tells us, so as to keep out of sight while Oxford wrote and published the plays. Yet it was after 1597, in 1598-1599, that Shakespeare played his leading role in hijacking the *Theatre*; in 1602-1604 that he was living in the Mountjoy home in London; and in 1608, as Cuthbert Burbage tells us, he was still one of the "men Players" of the Company. For Looney to claim he was permanently out of London by 1597 is merely untenable.

In instance after instance, having no evidence to support his Oxfordian claims, Looney goes to amazing extremes as he tries to show that many of the plays are autobiographical for Oxford. Any one instance will show the fantasy in which he indulged.

The play *Othello*, he tells us, is a striking parallel of Oxford's life. In the play the father-in-law of Othello is the chief minister of state; and in reality the father-in-law of Oxford was Cecil, Elizabeth's chief minister of state. Oxford went traveling in Europe and wrote home says Looney, "a warm regard for his wife" who was Cecil's daughter. Shortly thereafter Cecil (Elizabeth's chief minister) summoned Oxford home—but upon his arrival Oxford refused to see his wife, and "reports unfavorable to" the wife's reputation "gained currency." A servant of Oxford's, says Looney, "had succeeded in insinuating into" Oxford's "mind suspicions of some kind respecting" the wife. Thus the servant in real life is the Iago of the play. Then, says Looney, on page 229, as he struggles to prove the play is all autobiography:

> "It is worth while remarking that Othello was called back from Cyprus: the very part of the world which Oxford was prevented from visiting by his recall; and that he was called back to Venice, the city which Oxford had just left."

Just what that proves he fails to tell us. Also, he doesn't tell us why Oxford skipped past the autobiographical part and made Othello a Moor; and fortunately the real life parallel stopped before the protagonist, as in the play, committed suicide.

He struggles also to make *Hamlet* autobiographical. Oxford, he tells us, page 407, had a cousin named Horace de Vere, adding, "or, as the older records give it, Horatio de Vere." As Oxford was writing *Hamlet,* so Looney says, he decided that the fact that he himself was the true "Shakespeare" must be told to the public immediately after his death—"he had decided that these honours should be claimed on his behalf immediately after his death, and that Horatio de Vere had been entrusted with the responsibility." Accordingly, in writing *Hamlet,* Oxford gave as a name for Hamlet's closest friend "Horatio," and had Hamlet say to Horatio:

> "Absent thyself from felicity awhile,
> And in this harsh world draw thy breath
>   in pain, to tell my story."

This is all proved, Looney says, by the fact that Oxford's cousin Horace had (in the "older records') been called "Horatio." Or, to let Looney speak for himself (p. 408):

> "And as Horatio was the man selected by Hamlet to 'tell his story', the theory we put forward, that 'Shakespeare' had instructed his cousin Horatio de Vere to 'report him and his cause

aright to the unsatisfied,' is not without very substantial grounds."

Why, then, didn't Cousin Horatio *tell* his story, if there was any story to tell? And if Oxford had a story he wanted told "immediately after his death," why did he not tell it in a document to be opened posthumously?

It is for this sort of wild-blue-yonder theorizing that Looney asks us to brush aside the explicit testimony of Leonard Digges, Ben Jonson, Heminges, Condell and others, and accept Oxford as the author—"forget for awhile the thing called evidence."

Since Oxford died in 1604, and since for about eight years after that new Shakespearean plays kept coming out, the Oxfordians are hard put to it to explain how that could have happened. But their imaginations are equal to the occasion.

In or about 1592 Oxford more or less permanently disappeared from public view. That, says Looney (page 328), was because "he felt the necessity of seclusion, and a freedom from a sense of working under the public eye." Having perfected his writing ability, having learned all about the technicalities of the theatre, he went for twelve years into seclusion so that (page 327) he could "work upon his stores of incompleted dramas, giving them a more poetic form and a higher poetic finish." Not one scintilla of evidence is given to support this sheer theorizing.

In other words, Oxford remained in seclusion and polished his plays, letting them come out one by one for all twelve of those years between his disappearance in 1592 and his death in 1604, years in which the Shakespearean plays were illuminating the London stage, with all the glory going to that fraudulent man from Stratford.

Then, in 1604, when he died, he left the remainder of his plays in partially finished form, for lesser hands to finish and give out to the public one by one.

The *American Bar Association Journal* (September, 1959, page 941) also tells us this, and then adds the truly astounding information that the plays, before Oxford's final revision of them, were first *"performed in simple versions at court"!* One cannot help wondering who "performed" them—surely not the Chamberlain's Company. And one certainly would like to see a tiny bit of the evidence on which that amazing statement was based.

Othello, King Lear, Anthony and Cleopatra, Coriolanus, Timon of Athens, Cymbeline, Winter's Tale, The Tempest and *Henry VIII*, are all believed by scholars to have been written after 1604, when Oxford died—some demonstrably were. These, the Oxfordians would have us believe, were finished off by others and released one by one—strangely enough, without one word or even hint of it leaking out.

These are the theories, wholly unsupported, for which the Oxfordians ask us to "forget for a while the thing called evidence."

C.

Christopher Marlowe

Christopher Marlowe, born in 1564, as was Shakespeare of Stratford, was the son of a cobbler, but early showed himself a brilliant and greatly gifted person. Scholarships sent him through Corpus Christi College, Cambridge, where he received both B.A. and M.A. degrees.

A certain mystery exists regarding one incident during his university career, when he left and visited France, with the University on his return being informed by Privy Council itself that the visit to France had been in the interests of his country. It is generally believed that he went to France as a Government spy in the employ of Sir Francis Walsingham, head of Elizabeth's Secret Service.

Immediately upon leaving the University, he went to London, where he began writing plays with instantaneous success. Within a very short while he had gained the patronage of Sir Thomas Walsingham, cousin of Sir Francis, famous as a patron of the arts.

A man of obviously fiery and resentful nature, Marlowe brought his own troubles upon himself by ostentatiously and daringly flaunting his agnostic convictions, despite the fact that under Queen Elizabeth agnosticism was punishable by burning at the stake. With Catholic Spain an ever present threat, and with Catholic Mary Queen of Scots making claims for the English throne, affirmative Protestantism was more or less a requisite of a long life in the England of that day.

By May, 1593, Marlowe had gotten himself into serious trouble. On May 20th he was summoned before Privy Council on charges of agnosticism. He was not, however, immediately imprisoned but was ordered to report daily to Privy Council till decision was reached as to how to deal with him.

That decision was never reached, for within ten days Marlowe was officially dead. For some years a considerable mystery existed as to just how he had died. In a poem published in 1593 Gabriel Harvey had stated that he had died of the plague, then raging in London; but in 1597 Thomas Beard published a book, *The Theatre of God's Judgments,* stating that Marlowe had been murdered in London's streets. Then in 1600 William Vaugham in his *Golden Grove* published the true facts, i.e., that he had been murdered at Deptford, a little village three miles out of London. Nothing further of any contemporary nature was made public, but in 1820 one James Broughton, having read the report that the murder occurred in Deptford, wrote a letter to the rector of St. Nicholas Parish Church in that town and asked if there was any record of Marlowe's burial. That brought the reply that the Church's Register of Burials showed that Marlowe had been buried there on June 1, 1593, though his actual grave was never identified.

There the matter rested for another one hundred and five years. Naturally enough, the man who finally found the official document that purportedly cleared the mystery was none other than Dr. Leslie Hotson. In 1925, in the archives of the London Public Record Office, so frequently Dr. Hotson's happy hunting ground, he discovered the original copy of the Coroner's Inquest, to which was attached the killer's pardon signed in her own hand by Queen Elizabeth herself.

That document, written in Latin and drawn up by William Danby, "Coroner to the Household of our Lady the Queen," reported that Marlowe had been stabbed to death by one Ingram Frizer on May 30, 1593, in a room in the house of a Deptford widow named Eleanor Bull. Present at the time had been Nicholas Skeres and Robert Poley, and the killing had occurred after the four men had both dined and eaten supper there, an argument having then begun "about the payment of the sum of pence, that is, the recknynge there."

An inquest was held, with sixteen witnesses viewing the body of Marlowe. Frizer having satisfied the officials that he had killed Marlowe in self-defense, the Queen pardoned him on June 28, 1593.

This seemed to settle the matter, but in 1955 Mr. Calvin Hoffman published his *The Murder of the Man Who Was Shakespeare*, and presented to the world Christopher Marlowe as the author of the Shakespearean works, the fifty-seventh pretender in direct line.

Since the official record showed Marlowe dead on May 30, 1593, and since no one had ever reported seeing Marlowe otherwise than as a ghost since that date, Mr. Hoffman obviously had a sizeable problem on his hands to make his story stick. His story of how Marlowe wasn't really murdered but was spirited off to Europe has considerable inventive ingenuity and demonstrates quite clearly that Mr. Hoffman himself, at any rate, is quite convinced of his accuracy.

Marlowe, he points out, was a friend of Mr. Thomas Walsingham, whose vast country estate lay twelve miles outside London. Walsingham, though of noble ancestry with a cousin in the Queen's council, was demonstrably involved in wide intrigue— intrigue not to help his Government but to help himself and his wife to large quantities of ill-gotten pounds sterling. Remarkably enough, Ingram Frizer, the murderer, and his companions in the murder, Skeres and Poley, were all a part of Walsingham small army of privately kept crooks. And, more remarkable still, on the very day after his pardon by Queen Elizabeth, Ingram Frizer, the murderer, was once more back with Walsingham, actually living at his country estate.

This, surely, is enough to shake our confidence in Walsingham's complete integrity. But Mr. Hoffman goes further. Marlowe is sometimes believed to have been a homosexual, and it is Mr. Hoffman's theory that it was not merely his literary talents that grappled him to the soul of Walsingham, his patron and friend.

Seeing his beloved Marlowe in mortal danger, runs Mr. Hoffman's argument, Mr. Thomas Walsingham decided to take matters into his own hands. He spirited Marlowe out of London, where he was free on some sort of bail, took him out to his country estate and there the two of them cooked up a plan to frustrate the Privy Council and get Marlowe out of England. From this point on, Mr. Hoffman's story has to (and does) become complicated in the extreme, because he had so many facts of record that he was compelled to make use of.

For example, there was that dead body, viewed by sixteen jurors. It would never do to say Walsingham took the simple course and merely slipped Marlowe out of the country. That would leave that dead body unexplained. So Mr. Hoffman gives us a far more complicated plan, possibly more from necessity

than from choice. No indeed, Walsingham didn't take the obvious
and simple course of just shipping Marlowe off incognito; he
shipped him off incognito, Mr. Hoffman tells us, but he also
plotted to have his stooges Ingram Frizer *et al.* kill some poor
unknown fellow in Deptford, show that dead body to the Queen's
Coroner and to those sixteen jurymen, and tell the world that
Marlowe was dead—and then fool all posterity while Marlowe,
safely abroad, wrote Shakespearean play after Shakespearean
play and sent them back to Walsingham for production in London. One cannot find fault with Mr. Hoffman if his story gets
complicated; he *had* to make it complicated so as to explain all
the known facts.

Possibly it is best to let Mr. Hoffman himself tell of the plan.
At page 96 of his *Murder of the Man Who Was Shakespeare*
(Universal Library Edition), he describes it as follows, Scad-
bury Park being Walsingham's country estate:

> "At Scadbury Park the plans for Marlowe's escape mature. He
> must leave the country. The chance that someone would recog-
> nize him after the murder is one that cannot be taken. Not only
> Marlowe's life, Walsingham's and his accomplices' lives are in
> peril. The night before the Deptford murder the dramatist, dis-
> guised, will take the horse to Dover and embark across the
> Channel to France . . .
>
> "The two men say good-bye. The morning of the 30th dawns.
>
> "Marlowe is already in Dover—a 'dead' man fleeing to
> France. Frizer and Skeres are in Deptford. Early that morning
> they stroll the town"—and find a victim, possibly a sailor just
> off a ship. They lure him to Eleanor Bull's house and kill him,
> their story all ready for the Coroner.

It would have been so much simpler for Walsingham, instead
of risking his neck by becoming involved in a murder, merely
to have given Marlowe money and a horse and sent him on his

way. But no, with the dead man to be explained Mr. Hoffman had to choose his far more complicated story. And since the crooks were all demonstrably in Walsingham's permanent employ, a far simpler explanation of what happened seems easy. Possibly Walsingham, with Marlowe about to be tried, realized that he himself might be involved—and hence, to get rid of Marlowe, simply had his own hierlings kill him.

And, if Walsingham were truly risking his own life to save Marlowe for all those future plays, why didn't he just have Marlowe assume a fictitious *nom-de-plume?* Why go to all that trouble of hiring Shakespeare of Stratford to front for him? Obviously, if Marlowe wrote the plays, Shakespeare of Stratford could not for long fool his fellow actors. A *nom-de-plume* would have made everything so much simpler. That, however, would kill off Mr. Hoffman's theory—and kill off Marlowe as a pretender.

Venus and Adonis, Mr. Hoffman tells us, had already, in April, been registered in the Stationer's Registry, but without the author's name. In September, 1593, it was published as William Shakespeare's—so, if Mr. Hoffman's tale is correct, Walsingham acted with amazing speed in lining Shakespeare of Stratford up to carry on the hoax. He had to do it all between the murder, on May 30th, and the publication in September. Furthermore, the printer was Richard Field, who had grown up in Stratford with William Shakespeare. How convince *him?* Did Walsingham have to let him in on the plot?

And how was it that Meres wrote in 1598 that Shakespeare was circulating his "sugred sonnets among his private friends"? How does Mr. Hoffman explain that one away? Or why does the author in Sonnet 136 say, "my name is 'Will' "?

Mr. Hoffman, to explain away as much of the evidence as he can, tells us the usual stuff about the *First Folio*—how fraudulent it is. He would have us "forget for a while" the explicit testimony of Leonard Digges, Ben Jonson, Heminges, Condell and others, forget the Stratford monument with its words carved in stone, and believe instead the story he tells. No doubt those who are so inclined will do so.

XV

It Was Shakespeare of Stratford Who Was the Author

THE documented record shows beyond doubt or question that it was Shakespeare of Stratford who was the author.

The dreamt-up theories which our anti-Stratfordian friends ask us to accept, in lieu of the documented evidence, collapse of their own weight on thoughtful scrutiny. For those theories ask us to believe that the Stratford man was a fraud. Had he been a fraud he could never have carried it off for over twenty years— nor could the "great conspirators" have done it. The human reactions of the people around him would have prevented it.

For the name "William Shakespeare" early became famous in London, and the fame lasted throughout his lifetime and afterwards; and since there was no other "William Shakespeare" known to the public, all the public kudos of that fame had to center on him, the man from Stratford. Had he been a fraud his contemporaries would never have silently stood for that. Jealousy would have prevented it.

That great fame and glory shone on Shakespeare of Stratford during his lifetime is no dreamt-up fantasy. It is clearly proven by the fame and glory that was demonstrably heaped upon his memory after death.

Upon his death the poet William Basse suggested that he be buried in Westminster Abbey. His poem with that suggestion is printed in *Chambers,* Vol. II, p. 226, and is dated by Sir Edmund Chambers as having been written between 1616 and 1623. It said, in part:

> He dyed in April, 1616. "On Mr. Wm. Shakespeare
>
> Renowned Spencer, lye a thought more nye
> To learned Chaucer, and rare Baumont lye
> A little nearer Spenser to make roome
> For Shakespeare in your threefold foverfold Tombe."

Since Basse gave the date of Shakespeare's death as "April, 1616," it is impossible for our anti-Stratfordian friends to claim (as they so often do) that the reference in the name "Shakespeare" is not to the Stratford man but to some great unknown. Even so, the Ogburns (*Shakespeare, The Real Man Behind the Name,* page 155), tell us that Basse's poem was merely part of the "plot."

And shortly after his death came the Stratford monument, followed by the *First Folio* with all its praise. If the "great conspirators" were, as our anti-Stratfordian friends would have us believe, doing all that to fool the public as to the authorship, they could not have suddenly started it at his death. It had to have been going on earlier, for suddenly to have started it at his death with nothing said about it in his lifetime would have fooled no one.

The name "William Shakespeare" became famous almost overnight, upon the publication of *Venus & Adonis* in 1593 and *The Rape of Lucrece* in 1594. Hardly were they published before contemporary writers began hailing them, and hailing "William Shakespeare," as great. *Venus & Adonis* went through ten editions in Shakespeare's lifetime, and for awhile *The Rape of Lucrece* seemed even more popular, going through four editions in six years. An anthology published near the end of the 1590s contained ninety-one quotations from *Lucrece*. (Rowse, *William Shakespeare*, page 159; Chute, *Shakespeare of London*, page 117.)

Thus a great and popular light shone upon the name "William Shakespeare," and so far as the public knew there was only one, the actor from Stratford.

In 1598 Richard Barnfield wrote of "Shakespeare":

> "Whose *Venus*, and whose *Lucrece*
> (sweete and chaste)
> Thy Name in fame's immortal Booke
> have plac't."

And the next year John Weever urged him to "woo" his muse further, saying:

> "Honie-tong'd *Shakespeare* when I saw thine issue,
> I swore *Apollo* got them and none other,
> Their rosie-tainted features cloth'd in tissue,
> Some heaven born goddesse said to be their mother!
> Faire fire-hot *Venus* charming him to love her,
> Rose-checkt *Adonis* with his amber tresses,
> Chaste *Lucretia* virgine-like her dresses,
> Prowd lust-stung *Tarquine* seeking still to prove her
>
> . . .
>
> They burn in love thy children *Shakespear* het them,
> Go, wo thy Muse more Nymphish brood beget them."

Many others, including William Covell, Gabriel Harvey, Francis Meres and others, wrote in similar vein, all printed by Sir Edmund Chambers (*Chambers*, Vol. II, pages 190 et seq.).

Our anti-Stratfordian friends ask us to believe that all these writers, in praising "William Shakespeare," were praising some "great unknown." They have no evidence to support that theory but claim there is no evidence to refute it—the documented evidence that all this while there was only one "William Shakespeare" in the public eye, in London, namely, the actor from Stratford.

Is it conceivable (especially in the small city that Elizabethan London was) that those writers, hailing the emergence of a new talent, would have been hailing some "great unknown" and shown no curiosity as to who he was? Would they not at the very least have wanted him identified? Does a writer like John Weever urge this new and talented writer to "woo thy muse" —and not know who he was, or at least who he *thought* he was? Obviously, since no "William Shakespeare" was publicly known anywhere in London except William Shakespeare the actor, all those writers must have thought the actor was the writer—or else every one of them had been in on the "plot," as our anti-Stratfordian friends claim they all were. But does it make sense to say that all those writers would, so far as the public was concerned, be heaping praises upon the actor, the only "William Shakespeare" the public knew, when all the while the writers were in on the "plot" and knew he was a fraud? Are writers like that? Wouldn't some of them have managed to let the secret out?

Or, leaving the writers, consider his fellow actors. As the name "William Shakespeare" thus grew in fame in London, with the actor from Stratford the only "William Shakespeare" anyone knew of, hence in most eyes necessarily getting all the glory, would his fellow actors not have resented it and been jealous?

But instead they accepted him into their midst, acted with him, hi-jacked a theatre with him, left him at least one bequest in their wills with evidence of warmest affection, and once, in his Gate-House purchase, acted as trustee for him. For more than twenty years they took him to their bosoms; and then, after his death, perpetuated and immortalized his name in the *First Folio* which their last surviving two brought out "to keepe the memory of so worthy a Friend & Fellow alive, as was our Shakespeare, by humble offer of his playes."

"Forget for a while that evidence" our anti-Stratfordian friends urge, "and believe instead our theory wholly unsupported that the *First Folio* was all a hoax to deceive the public, with those actors lying for some small pay."

And never one whisper of the conspiracy leaked out—never one writer or one jealous actor said one single word!

Truly, it is the theories of our anti-Stratfordian friends that "contravene human experience." It is those theories, not the Stratford man's authorship, that are "impossible."

But it is unnecessary to argue the hollowness of the anti-Stratfordian theories. The affirmative documented evidence destroys their every claim.

At times our anti-Stratfordian friends put forward the assertion that there is no proof that Shakespeare of Stratford and Shakespeare the London actor were one and the same man. But the documents thoroughly knock that argument out.

Of primary, and overwhelming, importance on that point is the priceless document that emerged in 1602 when Ralph Brooke, the York Herald, accused some of his fellow Heralds of being too easy in the granting of coats-of-arms, citing as an instance the granting of a coat-of-arms to John Shakespeare, William's father. Fortunately that document is still extant and is now in the Folger Library in Washington. There, on that document (see frontispiece), is set forth a drawing of the Stratford Shakespeare coat-of-arms and under it, thought to be in Brooke's handwriting, are the words "Shakespear ye Player." This irrefutably shows that Shakespeare the player was Shakespeare of Stratford.

That proof is further supplemented by the bequests in Shakespeare's will to his "fellowes John Hemmynge, Richard Burbage and Henry Cundell" and by the *First Folio's* calling him

135

the Sweet Swan of Avon, and "Stratford moniment." Our anti-Stratfordian friends attempt to discredit the bequests and the *First Folio,* but are helpless in front of the evidence in the document that emerged from the Heralds' fight. Shakespeare of Stratford and Shakespeare the player were demonstrably one and the same man.

The documented proof that he was the author started early and built to a crushing climax.

In 1593 came *Venus & Adonis,* published by Richard Field, his neighbor from Stratford, who stated that the book was written by William Shakespeare—and Field was in position to know. The name could not have been a *nom-de-plume,* for none of the pretenders had ever used a *nom-de-plume* and had no reason to use one on that non-political poem. Nor is it conceivable that had they chosen a *nom-de-plume* they would have chosen not only the last name but the first name also of the man from Stratford then acting on the London stage.

Furthermore, and most overwhelming proof of all, there is the dedication of the book to the Earl of Southampton—in words not one of the pretenders would ever have used but which fit the Stratford man like a glove.

Venus & Adonis was followed by *The Rape of Lucrece,* piling up similar evidence of his authorship.

In the year 1598 Francis Meres, in his *Palladis Tamia,* credits "Shakespeare" with the authorship of the twelve plays named there. That he was referring to Shakespeare of Stratford is inescapable, because he tells us that the Shakespeare there mentioned was circulating "his sugred sonnets among his private friends." That necessarily eliminates every possibility that Meres was referring to some pretender, for not one of the pretenders could have circulated the sonnets as "Shakespeare's" without instantly giving away the secret of the hidden authorship. Meres also mentions Marlowe and Oxford as well as Shakespeare, and mentions them as three separate men. *Palladis*

Tamia alone is proof that Shakespeare of Stratford was the author.

Then in 1615 comes proof that no anti-Stratfordian theory can explain away or avoid, namely, the recently discovered letter from Beaumont, the playwright, to Ben Jonson, written not for publication. It is a private communication between two playwrights who could not possibly have failed to know "William Shakespeare," whoever he was, and in it Beaumont tells us that Shakespeare lacked scholarship and went far "by the dimme light of nature." He could not possibly have been referring to any pretender, only to Shakespeare of Stratford, for the words fit no one else.

Then comes his Stratford monument, with words carved in stone by his contemporaries, stating that he it was who was the writer. The anti-Stratfordian efforts to discredit this titanic piece of evidence are merely grotesque.

And then, in 1623, comes the *First Folio*, where Heminges and Condell, Leonard Digges and Ben Jonson, all of whom knew him or knew well who he was, all tell us that Shakespeare of Stratford wrote the plays.

The anti-Stratfordian attempts to discredit the *First Folio* are, if our friends will again pardon our use of the word, merely silly. To "forget for a while" the documented evidence of Leonard Digges, who grew up in Stratford, of Ben Jonson, who showed in his *Timber* what he thought of Shakespeare, and of Heminges and Condell, who were his fellow actors for over twenty years, would be to blind ourselves to history. There is no shred of evidence that discredits the *First Folio*—merely those theories, unsupported, that spring from wishful thinking.

And then, when almost fifty years had passed, we learn from the Reverend John Ward, Rector of Shakespeare's Stratford church, that Shakespeare's reputation in Stratford is still so great that he as Rector must "peruse" the plays himself so that "I may not be ignorant in that matter."

The *American Bar Association Journal,* in its issue of November, 1959, page 1225, makes this statement to the lawyers of America:

> "If the First Folio were eliminated, there would be no evidence whatever even remotely purporting to connect Shaksper, the man from Stratford, with Shakespeare, the author."

The Ogburns make a similar statement in their *Shakespeare, The Real Man Behind The Name,* p. 150.

Odd that they would say such a thing when all the while the Stratford monument, with those original words carved in stone, was staring them straight in the face. However, argument is pointless. A mere glance at the documented evidence shows that even without the *First Folio,* the proof that he was the writer is overwhelming.

Convinced, as they so obviously are, that "It is impossible that that Stratford man was the author," our anti-Stratfordian friends are really beyond the reach of evidence, no matter how well documented. "Come with us," they say, "into Anti-Stratfordia, our little world of fantasy. Forget for awhile the thing called evidence, and dream awhile with us."

Charming, self-deluded lotus-eaters, we shall continue to hear from them as we have in the past.

Addenda

YOUR true anti-Stratfordian, convinced as he is that the Stratfordian authorship is "impossible," has long shown himself adept at bringing craftily hidden meanings out of simple English sentences by means of strained interpretations.

A few instances of this have come to light since this book went to press.

I

That In Saying, In Sonnet 136, "My Name Is Will," the Author Was Secretly Saying "My Name Is De Vere, Earl of Oxford."

As we have seen, *supra*, in Sonnet 136, the author, in simple English words, told us "My name is 'Will'."

Our Oxfordian friends, however, give those words a different meaning. There was (or at least so they tell us) an Elizabethan word "wyl", which meant "spring" or "brook". Going from there into Latin, they tell us that the Latin word for "spring" is "ver", hence the author was really saying "My name is 'Ver' "—from which point the transition to "de Vere"—hence the "Earl of Oxford"—is easy.

The author, of course, did not say "My name is wyl." He

said "My name is 'Will'," and in saying it he used a capital W and put the name "Will" in quotation marks. Could he have told us more clearly that his name was "Will," which was an abbreviation of "William"?

And look further—the Sonnets tell us not only that the *author's* name was "Will"; they tell us also that his young *friend's* name was "Will." As the Ogburns themselves point out on page 82 of their *Shakespeare, The Real Man Behind the Name*: "Both he and the young man were known as 'Will'."

So, since by their own interpretation of the Sonnets, "Will" in the Sonnets means "wyl" which means "spring" which via Latin means "ver" which means "de Vere", then on their own interpretation the young friends name also was "de Vere". Truly, all roads lead to Rome. He was surely not Oxford's son. Just which de Vere was he?

It is into such bogs that harshly strained interpretations lead.

II

That Beaumont's Words, "By the Dimme Light of Nature," Can Be Rationalized Away Via that Great Elizabethan "Plot."

As we have seen *supra*, Beaumont, in his letter to Ben Jonson in 1615, said what appeared to mean that Shakespeare went far "by the dimme light of nature." But see what Mr. Charlton Ogburn, Jr. does to those words.

In his recent brochure *Shakespeare and the Man From Stratford*, Mr. Ogburn says, page 29:

> "In a neat bit of poetical double-talk addressed to Jonson, the playwright Francis Beaumont had shown he was on to the plan to have it appear that Shakespeare was an uneducated man:
>
> Here I would let slip
> (If I had any in me) scholarship,

And from all learning keep these lines as clear
As Shakespeare's best are, which our heirs shall hear
Preachers apt to their auditors to show
How far sometimes a mortal man may go
By the dim light of nature.

Beaumont did not say, as we are asked to believe by Stratfordians like Louis Marder and James G. McManaway, that
Shakespeare's lines are clear of learning; he said his *best*
ones are, with tongue-in-cheek implications that his others
are not. He did not say, as we are asked to believe, that
Shakespeare showed how far a man may go by the dim light
of nature; he said that is what posterity will be *told* by preachers apt ("suited, fitted, adapted") to their audiences. And
how right he was."

Here we see strained interpretation blossoming into its
fullest flower.

If Beaumont really meant merely that preachers would tell
the fraudulent story to their auditors, then Mr. Ogburn himself has used the precise word to describe his own interpretation—"double-talk." Beaumont, he tells us, was in on the
great "plot," hence his clear language is to be interpreted as
"double-talk." Of course, Mr. Ogburn has not the slightest
scintilla of evidence to show that any such "plot" existed, or
could have existed; nor any evidence to show that Beaumont
even *thought* such a "plot" existed.

Still, says Mr. Ogburn, we must read Beaumont's statement
as "double-talk." Why?

Surely that joke which the insiders were playing on the
public, by pretending that that ignorant man from Stratford
was the author, must have grown a little stale by 1615. It
had to have begun at least by 1592; hence Ben Jonson by
1615 must have heard it hundreds of times. Hardly likely
that he would laugh uproariously in 1615 at Beaumont's little
"double-talk." Why did Beaumont hand it to him?

Such strained interpretations are the stock-in-trade of every
anti-Stratfordian. Indeed, without them they would be unable

141

to keep themselves in the public eye. When clear, simple language, testifying to the Stratford man's authorship, faces them, they cry "Double-talk!"—or else insist that the witness was lying for pay. Thus Heminges, Condell, Leonard Digges, Beaumont, Ben Jonson, the Stratford Monument, King James, and even Shakespeare himself (whoever he was) were all engaging in "double-talk"—or else were simply lying, and never, never, so much as one scintilla of evidence to support the charge or justify the strained interpretations! Yet they ask us to accept them!

III

That the Dark Lady of the Sonnets
Was Anne Vavasor, Lady-in-Waiting
to the Queen and Intimate Friend of Oxford.

Here again our anti-Stratfordian friends are asking us to forget for a while the thing called evidence.

For the Sonnets clearly show that the Dark Lady was no Lady-in-Waiting to the Queen.

Say the Ogburns in their *Shakespeare, The Real Man Behind the Name,* on page 88:

> "The Dark Lady would presumably be Anna Vavasor, a brunette wanton with whom Oxford had an affair."

Previously, on page 72, they told us that Anne was "one of the Queen's maids" and, on page 15, that the Queen "was enraged when he had a love affair with the attractive brunette, Anna Vavasor."

In fact, on pages 241-242 of their book the Ogburns quote in full Oxford's poem which they entitle "Anna Vavasor's Echo," in which Oxford says that he "knew this lady well."

Well, if Anne Vavasor was the Dark Lady, why do the Sonnets tell us that the Dark Lady seduced not only Shakespeare (whoever he was) but his young friend as well? If she circulated as widely as that, why was the Queen "enraged" at Oxford?

Also, if Anne Vavasor, a Lady-in-Waiting, was the Dark Lady, why did Shakespeare (whoever he was) tell us so clearly that the Dark Lady was a prostitute, "the bay where all men ride," "the wide world's common place"? And why minutely describe the Dark Lady as he did?

Thus we have Sonnet 137, addressed to the Dark Lady, saying:

> "Thou blind fool, love, what dost thou to mine eyes
> That they behold and see not what they see?
> They know what beauty is, see where it lies,
> Yet what the best is take the worst to be.
> If eyes, corrupt by over-partial looks,
> Be anchored in the bay where all men ride,
> Why of eyes' falsehood hast thou forged hooks
> Whereto the judgment of my heart is tied?
> Why should my heart think that a several plot
> Which my heart knows the wide world's common place?
> Or mine eyes seeing this, say this is not,
> To put fair truth upon so foul a face?"

And in Sonnet 130 we have the following description of the Dark Lady:

> "My mistress' eyes are nothing like the sun,
> Coral is far more red than her lips red;
> If snow be white, why then her breasts are dun,
> If haires be wires, black wires grow on her head.
> I have seen roses damasked, red and white,
> But no such roses see I in her cheeks;
> And in some perfumes is there more delight
> Than in the breath that from my mistress reeks.
> I love to hear her speak, yet well I know
> That music hath a far more pleasing sound;
> I grant I never saw a goddess go:
> My mistress, when she walks, treads on the ground."

Hardly words written by the noble Oxford about a Lady-in-Waiting to the Queen.

IV

That the Opening Line of Sonnet 125 Proves that the Earl of Oxford Was the Author.

The opening line of Sonnet 125 reads as follows:

"Were't aught to me I bore the canopy."

"There!" exclaim our Oxfordian friends, "That word 'canopy' is our proof—proof as clear as a summer's day that the Earl of Oxford was the author!"

Their theory is that at some great occasion Oxford (so they claim) was one of those who bore a canopy over Queen Elizabeth, and that in that opening line he is referring back to that great occasion, his meaning being "Were't aught to me I bore the canopy over Queen Elizabeth." And clearly, if the opening line refers to a canopy borne over Queen Elizabeth, it could not have been Shakespeare of Stratford who bore it.

Hence, they say, that word "canopy" eliminates the Stratford man and points the finger clearly at the Earl of Oxford.

No doubt that argument would have strength if it were clear that the author is referring to a canopy borne over Queen Elizabeth—but who says that is what the author is referring to? Nobody—except the hard-pressed Oxfordians.

Sonnet 125 is the one hundred twenty-fifth Sonnet in unbroken sequence addressed to the young man the author is urging to get married. Having just addressed one hundred twenty-four Sonnets to him, discussing varied aspects of his unmarried state, why would the author begin the one hundred twenty-fifth to him by asking if it were aught to the author that he, the author, bore the canopy "over Queen Elizabeth?" It makes little, if any, sense, and seems to mangle the lines that follow.

The first four lines of Sonnet 125 read as follows:

"Were't aught to me I bore the canopy,
  With my extern the outward honouring,
  Or laid great bases for eternity,
  Which prove more short than waste or ruining?"

Would Oxford have written *those* lines with *Queen Elizabeth* in mind?

If Oxford wrote that first line he must also have written the next three. Having said (on their interpretation) "Were't aught to me I bore the canopy over Queen Elizabeth," he then went on to add "I was only outwardly honouring her, and though I laid foundations that should have lasted forever they have proven to be disappointingly short." Hardly what the author was saying, since he was addressing the Sonnet to the young man. Why would he have said it? And, furthermore, would the noble Oxford, courtier that he was, have talked that way about the Queen?

Most scholars (our hard-pressed Oxfordian friends excepted) agree that the lines above quoted mean "Were it aught to me I bore the canopy over you (the young man), outwardly honouring you and laying foundations for a relationship that should have lasted forever but has now proved disappointingly short." (See Rowse, *Shakespeare's Sonnets*, page 259; Dr. Leslie Hotson, *Mr. W. H.*, page 37.) That interpretation seems clearly borne out by the fact that with Sonnet 125 the Sonnets to the young man abruptly cease. Shakespeare, for reasons now unknown, was through with him, and in Sonnet 125 was telling him so, with great dignity.

"But," say our Oxfordian friends, "how explain that word 'canopy' if it wasn't a canopy borne over the Queen?"

In Elizabethan times the word "canopy" frequently did indicate royalty. No mere lord or earl was privileged to walk abroad with a tangible canopy borne over him; that was reserved for regents. As Dr. Leslie Hotson puts it (*Mr. W. H.*, page 38), "when we look under carried canopies, we find none but princes, royalties."

So, taken in its literal, tangible sense "canopy" did indicate royalty. But Shakespeare didn't confine himself to that tangible meaning. He used it also in a metaphorical sense, as when he had Hamlet say (Act II, Scene II) "this most excellent canopy, the air."

Taken in a metaphorical sense the word as used in Sonnet 125 means that Shakespeare's immortal poetry gave the young man a status almost regal. For one hundred twenty-four consecutive Sonnets Shakespeare had immortalized the young man in deathless poetry—poetry which the poet himself said (Sonnet 18) would live "So long as men can breathe, or eyes can see," adding "and this gives life to thee;" then in Sonnet 125 he summed this up in metaphor, likening his poetry to a canopy over the young man, forever honouring him and elevating him to great royal heights.

That seems to be the interpretation generally given to that word "canopy" (see Rowse, *Shakespeare's Sonnets*, page 259). Dr. Hotson, however, has a different interpretation (see *Mr. W. H.*, page 38). There Dr. Hotson tells us who he believes the young man was, i.e., the young man of the Sonnets, referred to by the printer as *"Mr. W. H.".*

No one knows with complete assurance who the young man of the Sonnets was. Many believe he was the young Earl of Southampton, whose cause is championed by Mr. Rowse in his *Shakespeare's Sonnets*. But Dr. Hotson assures us in his *Mr. W. H.* that the young man was William Hatcliffe, a gay aristocratic young student at Gray's Inn. There in 1587-8 young Mr. Hatcliffe was crowned "Prince of Purpoole" in the vastly elaborate holiday gaieties put on by the young students at the Inns of Court. At those affairs, extending over many days, royalty was simulated, with all the royal trimmings including a canopy, and with rather compelling reasoning Dr. Hotson (*Mr. W. H.*, pages 37 et seq.) tells us that *that* was the canopy referred to in Sonnet 125.

146

In either case, the metaphorical meaning preferred by Mr. Rowse or the literal one preferred by Dr. Hotson, the "canopy" was held not over Queen Elizabeth but over the young man to whom the Sonnet is addressed, and no reason exists for dragging in Queen Elizabeth's name.

V

The Three Sonnets Whose Evidence Kills Off Every Pretender

Three of the Sonnets make it crystal clear that only Shakespeare of Stratford, the "upstart crow," could have been the author.

As we have seen above, in Sonnet 136 the author tells us "My name is Will"—and only the man from Stratford had the name "William."

In Sonnet 25 the author says:

> "Let those who are in favor with their stars
> Of public honour and proud titles boast,
> Whilst I, whom fortune of such triumph bars,
> Unlooked for joy in that I honour most."

Could it have been Oxford, bearing the proud title "Seventeenth Earl!" and on numerous occasions publicly honoured by the Queen (such as when he was appointd on of the judges in the trial of Essex), could it have been Oxford who thus so wrote of himself as one "whom fortune of such triumph bars"? Or could it have been Bacon, so greatly honoured with the proud title "Lord Chancellor of England"? Or was it the "upstart crow" from Stratford, who had no title and no public honours?

In Sonnet 78 the author refers to the Rival Poet (generally believed to have been Marlowe) as "learned" and compares him to himself and "my rude ignorance."

Could it have been the highly educated Oxford, the University graduate Marlowe, or Bacon, the most erudite man in England, who humbly referred to "my rude ignorance"?

Or was it the "upstart crow" from Stratford?

L'envoi

One parting thought should be held uppermost in the un-prejudiced reader's mind—namely, the absurdity of the anti-Stratfordians as they strive, without so much as one shred of evidence, to establish their great Elizabethan secret "plot," so wholly essential to every pretender's claims.

No pretender, writing those plays at the rate of two a year, could have personally delivered them to the actors—for the secrecy would at once have vanished. It had to be done by an intermediary.

But as each new play was delivered, rehearsed and shown to be an instantaneous hit, even the dullest actor must have begun to wonder "Who can the author be?" If the ostensible Shakespeare was a fraud, he would be instantly dismissed from the actors' minds, and even the stupidest man in the theatre would have seen that a huge plot of secrecy was being perpe-trated. That included not only every actor but every theatre hireling as well, for they too heard all the gossip.

And why would no one talk, with so intriguing a conversa-tional subject? The actors who played the female roles were boys of little more than twelve—necessarily so young that their voices had not changed. Would children as young as that, to

148

say nothing of the obscure hirelings who could instantly vanish, if necessary, be silenced by some rumored but unwritten injunction from the Royal Court?

Theatre people inevitably mingle with theatre people, and in the London of that day the theatre people numbered in the hundreds, some entire casts being exclusively young boys. As they mingled they inevitably talked theatre gossip—and in the London of that day, probably less than one-third the size of present-day Cambridge, Massachusetts, the gossip, if intriguing enough, would soon reach every ear in town.

Yet from 1592 to 1640, as all this hush-hush gossip went the rounds, it was kept totally bottled up—so much so that not even one recorded whisper of it leaked out, not even one.

Truly a strange phenomenon with which to brush aside documented evidence of such overwhelming volume.

Yet without this "plot" not one of the entire fifty-seven pretenders dares show his face.

Bibliographical Index

This section lists those plays, books and articles mentioned in the text.

Bibliographical Index

Subject Index

Index

Marlow = rebellious
Hyhedwatin
147